Black, Gay & Underage

Wil Roach

First print edition: Sydney, 2019.
First ebook edition: Sydney, 2019.
Publisher: Sydney School of Arts & Humanities
15-17 Argyle Place NSW 2000 Australia
www.ssoa.com.au

Black, Gay & Underage
ISBN: 978-0-6483216-5-1 (print book)
        978-0-6483216-6-8 (ebook)

What follows is a true story. The dates, place names and events in this memoir are factual. However, some names have been changed in order to protect privacy.
Cover design & formatting Ferdinando Manzo
Typeset Times New Roman
Printed and bound by Lightning Source, 2019.

National Library of Australia Cataloguing-in-Publication data:
Wil Roach, author, 2019.
Black, Gay & Underage / Roach, Wil.
ISBN   978-0-6483216-5-1 (print book)
        978-0-6483216-6-8 (ebook)

Dedication

with much love
to Dad and Mum
who never lost hope
and truly cared for whoever crossed their path.

Acknowledgements

My gratitude to Kristina Karasulas and the Redfern Community Centre Writers' Group who encouraged me to write at the beginning of my story. I'm also grateful to author Kate Howarth who engaged me in conversations about the craft of writing.

Thanks to Jason Roger Phillips and Veronica Hannon for giving me critical but supportive feedback, and to the Jones family, Gabrielle Journey, Sofara and Jai, whose enthusiasm on hearing my work propelled me forward.

I must also give thanks to members of the Friday Writing Group at Sydney School of Arts & Humanities for their gentle comments on my work.

My grateful acknowledgement to Paul Capsis for his enduring support and for always being present for me.

Contents

Introduction

When a ship dropped anchor in the English south coast port of Southampton, on a dull Saturday morning on the 31 August 1962, among the optimistic travellers were a Trinidadian mother and seven-month-old baby. By a peculiar set of circumstances only heaven could send, as they set foot on the soil of their colonial rulers for the previous three hundred years, the colony of Trinidad and Tobago ceased to be. The country had gained political and economic independence to conduct its own affairs among the assembly of free nation states.

It was my mother's and my first journey from the land of her birth. After a year of waiting and then travelling for three weeks by ship, followed by completion of the disembarkation checks, Shirley Angelina Roach carried her baby, Wilfred Carson Roach, in her arms down the ship's gangplank. Mother and baby had left Trinidad colonial citizens and now were arriving on the very day of Trinidad's independence. It was a peculiar set of circumstances being experienced in my young life – and there would be many more to follow. The scene would be one of the last to occur after mass migration had begun, at the end of the Second World War.

Anxiously awaiting their arrival at Southampton was Shirley's husband, the father of Wilfred, Clifford Wilfred Roach, along with his sister Carmen and her husband Norman Clarke. Clifford had made a considered decision to leave his colonial existence behind, embracing a future in what he thought of as 'the home country' – Great Britain.

Mother and child had voyaged some 8,000 miles, first across the warm Caribbean Sea and then an unpredictable Atlantic Ocean. Husband and wife had not seen each other in almost a year and had kept in touch by airmail letter. Clifford would see me, his baby son, for the first time.

Thus began a new and unpredictable chapter in this innocent baby's life, of twists and turns to come. His life was literally in the hands of Shirley and Clifford. Years later I would marvel at their fortitude and sangfroid in the face of what would become a living sentence for them, and for many who could only secretly count their small blessings living in Great Britain.

Shirley and Clifford made up a contrasting couple. She shorter and darker than him, with soft hair, and fiery of thought and deed. A proud Christian woman who had cared for her own niece like a mother before she'd even reached the age of twenty. My father was tall, with mahogany skin, beautiful hair, teeth and a solemn countenance. He spoke rarely at home except when he was in lecture mode, mostly silent in his thoughts. He too had cared for his grandmother and nephews before he left Trinidad to seek his destiny in 'merry' England. Clifford had a clear intention to study case law and return to his beloved Trinidad.

Shirley and her baby were both leaving whole existences behind with retinues of mothers, fathers, sisters, brothers, cousins, even my maternal grandmother and grandfather whose bonds with them were severed abruptly. Also left behind was the hardship engendered by the intellectual, economic and societal depredations of hundreds of years of colonial rule in Trinidad, first by the Spanish and last by the British.

In a poor exchange for tropical heat from a generous sun, the baby is given dark afternoons and an all-encompassing cold that eats into the very marrow of his bones as he grows.

The introduction of the boy to his home, a cold room in an ageing London suburb, is brutal – as if he is being prepared by surgeons for more radical surgery. The laboratory for this small black boy is school and as he grows older and becomes a teenager, the experiments take on a darker hue until he wonders if he has been forsaken by God and his parents, both.

As his comprehension expands, they cannot tell him if and when his life will get better. He just has to 'turn the other cheek' and 'work hard'. There are few distractions to keep him from losing his mind. No holidays away. No child's play. Nothing to show him what to look forward to as he agonises over teachers' slights. So he retreats into himself. Into a silence that requires no commitment beyond getting the immediate job done, as required by authority figures: parents, teachers and other adults.

By adolescence a new consciousness appears in the form of thoughts he has that silence is not the way, that he has to give voice to bring his hopes alive. He has to undertake a journey through the dread of his own terrors: will they like me, will they hate me, will they kill me? And will I amount to nothing at the end of my struggles? He prepares for his journey armed with his father's sayings: 'Walk quietly with a big stick,' and 'If you see a man coming towards you and he wants to fight, cross to the other side'.

The father dreamed of returning in triumph to Trinidad vindicated by his decision to leave that known but limited life that was Tunapuna. As his son grew, the father would repeat the mantra to 'turn the other cheek' to racism from his English brethren, because the coloniser and ex-colonial would never be equal, he believed.

On Sunday afternoons, Clifford would often say, 'Oil and water don't mix'. Well, he and Shirley put their baby in that water and what was the result? Let's see what came of this blend of musky Trinidadian and English brew.

Chapter 1
London in winter

The red Routemaster double-decker bus moved slowly through almost impenetrable sheets of snow obscuring the road ahead. I was unsure where we had come from or where we were going. It was 1964, and I was almost three. Daddy and I sat on the lower deck of the bus, he in his thick black coat and dark shoes and I with my knitted hat and an almost identical coat many sizes smaller, my red wellington boots, and a scarf fitted tight around my neck.

My mum had told me, 'This will protect you against the cold'. I had resented her intrusion, saying nothing as I gently pulled away from her act of kindness. I objected, without raising her ire.

Now I looked down at my warm trousers and shiny wellington boots with ridging on the soles. 'To help you walk, and not slide in the snow,' Mummy had said. The boots had been difficult to get on and a paralysis had taken hold of me.

'I can't do this!' I was close to tears.

'Come, stand still,' Mummy had said, asking me to steady my left leg, while she tugged the boot onto the right, and then the actions in reverse for the left. It was similar with round top jumpers; my head would get stuck and then I would be tugging furiously with frustration, only to be rescued by a calm, un-flappable mother, as if she'd done this a thousand times before.

While I was happy to receive the help, drawing unfavour-able attention to myself caused me worry. Mummy would in-sist that I wear certain items of clothing, none or very few of which would suit me, I felt, even from just a few years old. She'd hand me a pair of gloves with the ends cut off – mit-tens – saying, 'Hold your hands out,' as if I were to receive a punishment, roughly placing them over each finger of my two small hands.

'These will protect your hands from the cold weather.' At the end of this arduous process she'd sigh, 'There that's bet-ter!' as if to an invisible audience.

My thought was that I couldn't wait to grow up, to escape such impositions by adults. She would look me up and down, as if I was one of my toy soldiers, to ensure everything was just so, pulling at my hat to reach some invisible line that had not been followed. I wanted to get outside with Daddy because it was a rare treat for me to be with him alone.

On one particular day, I can't remember where or who we visited, but getting on the bus was a relief from the freezing conditions underfoot of slippery snow on the street. I felt se-cure with Daddy as he took the outside seat, leaving me secure and snug on the inside seat, my favourite spot as I could get a slightly better view out of the large bus window. I confidently blew warm air from my mouth to see thin vapours evaporating into cold air. The bus had a damp homely smell that stayed in my nostrils. I looked down between my legs and saw pools of water gathering in the narrow wooden floor grooves now dark-ened by the water from melting ice. I could see other people on our deck with their backs to me, such as a lady whose coat seemed to sparkle with drops of water where snowflakes had fallen and melted.

There was also a man in a dark uniform who had a silver machine with a black handle which I had seen before, when travelling with Mummy. The conductor would ask where we were going and then turn the black handle, which would provide the correct number of paper tickets for the passengers travelling.

On this trip, Dad paid for one ticket to a place I hadn't heard of before, 'Kilburn,' and then put his ticket in his pocket. I was miffed, as Mummy would always buy two tickets and give one to me, which I would carefully put in my pocket.

As the bus slowly churned through the mounds of snow, all I could hear was the noisy rumble of its engine. I occasionally glanced at Daddy but he continued to stare straight ahead. I wondered if he was asleep. His stillness affected me in comparison to Mummy's routine of always pointing things out to me in an observant manner. His silence left me nowhere to hide.

I watched the passing scenes outside, excited and hoping we could stay on the bus a long time. Then, without warning, Daddy reached up out of his seat, and with his left hand pulled the thin wire that ran the length of the bus's lower deck. This rang to tell the driver and conductor that a passenger wanted to get off at the next stop.

As the ringing from the wire cut the silence, Daddy got up, asking me to take his hand. The bus pulled up at an unfamiliar stop, with the bus conductor telling Daddy, 'Mind your step.'

Daddy seemed to hear but didn't respond as he lifted me off the bus without incident. Then he thanked the conductor as we stood on the pavement, and the bus moved off slowly into a misty gloom of falling snow.

Daddy then firmly took my hand in his and we walked away from the bus stop along a road with shops covered in snow. There were no vehicles about as we slowly trudged through the snow and turned a corner to see a row of houses covered in snow. I wondered where all the people had gone.

It continued to snow gently but without noise, so that the tranquillity of the scene disturbed me. I tried to listen to myself breathing and all I could see was white. I gripped Daddy's hand and although he didn't look at me, I knew he was there all the time. I wanted to ask him where we were going but didn't have the words.

I heard the crunch of my small feet on the snow, which seemed to be hardening. Cold was now attacking my face. I liked the sound but wanted to get out of the snow. I looked up at Daddy standing so tall, like a giant tree, as silent as his surroundings. I hoped he knew where we were going because I didn't. Without the language to ask him, the thought that he would know reassured me.

As we walked from the bus stop, Daddy was seemingly untouched by the snow, taking strides in his now sparkling black shoes, and wearing his coat tightly laced and a flat dark cap covering his enormous head, his ears poking out. *Where are we going? Where?* I wondered.

I looked up at my dad who, like those trees seemed to reach to the sky which was covered in white fluff. The snow seemed to muffle all sound except for the 'crunch, crunch' of our shoes and boots as they bit into the snow. Looking down at the stark white pavement, I saw a small impression of my boot so I stamped my foot a little harder with each step to make the same impression over and over in the snow.

Soon I grew impatient trudging through the snow. My eyes were closing and I became despondent as we seemed to have walked forever. I began to drag my feet too, as a signal to Daddy that I felt tired. Then, pointing my finger at the snow, I said in a whisper, 'Daddy, look! Dirty, dirty!' pointing at a cathedral shape of white snow at my feet mixed with grit, slowing my walk to a standstill. Daddy seemed not to slacken his pace at all as he smiled down at me and lifted me through the air as if I was flying before I landed in his arms. He laughed and proceeded to carry me the remaining distance.

In that moment I felt safe and happy. Daddy's pace slowed as we reached a gate and beyond that a snow-covered path leading up to a wood-and-glass door. The house was in darkness. Daddy, silent, gently steered me onto the path. He reached into his pocket and took out a key which he put in a lock, slowly turning it as if not wanting to make any noise. He took care to brush his shoes on the mat inside the hall and beckoned me to do the same.

We were now in the darkened hallway and I felt a chill wind brush against my back before he closed the front door behind us.

It was late at night and this was why the house seemed empty. It would be my home for the next few years and I would find out soon enough about the people who lived there and the rules for living, which it was imperative I follow.

Chapter 2
Beyond our room

As a child at home in Kilburn the days felt dull, with the outside gloom penetrating every corner of this old house that Mummy, Daddy and I called home. The winter days were short and the silence all-pervading. I would follow my mother around as she carried out her various chores in our bedroom, or the kitchen. I had no idea what she was doing but she was showing me, preparing me, for service. All my early days seemed like this. Then there was the phrase she and my father's sister, Auntie, whose home we lived in, always used: 'Spare the rod and spoil the child'. There was a language that was not spoken but tele-pathically communed between mother and son – that I was to be invisible and noiseless in a household of noisy adults and child cousins, as I was the baby of the two co-habiting fami-lies, the Clarkes and Roach's.

No questions of what I wanted were permitted, such as when I heard the tinkling of the ice cream van coming along our street. 'Now, you know not to ask for an ice cream. They're not good for your teeth.'

Yes, I understood never to ask for an ice cream. I knew to stifle my longing for the things I could see and wanted, such as toys or clothes, reinforced with the edict from Mummy that,

'Children are given and do not ask!'

There was a reward to my yearning for space not shared with family and that was to run around and make noise outside, and to see the sky. Mummy would ask me, 'Wilfred, do you want to go to the park?' My reply, 'Yes,' resembled that of a prisoner to a jailer in a voice so small it could hardly be heard by me, let alone Mummy. I yearned for freedom from the monotony, to be removed from the claustrophobic small room we called our own, in a big house that was not ours but belonged to Uncle and Auntie.

Mummy would dress me in our room, first in underwear, a white vest, a warm jumper, warm coat and lace-up shoes. Never outside of our room, where privacy and modest behaviour were emphasised; in other words, no running around naked in the house for me in summer. She would decide what I was to wear and then put the clothes on our bed. I had no say in it though I had some favourite items which Mummy without words would know and put out to please me. She told me that many of the clothes I wore, 'No longer fitted Charles,' who was the cousin closest in age to me. She and Auntie agreed that I could wear his clothes until I grew out of them, and it's a faint fear I hold to this day that I may have to wear clothes that are too tight or that I don't feel happy wearing. As I grew older, she would stand and watch me put on each item of clothing, including unpicking my laces for the umpteenth time with the words, 'This is how you do it, Wilfred,' but still it would make no sense to me.

Then it would be her turn, and she'd ask me to wait a moment while she dressed herself, which always seemed to take longer than time itself. She would sit in front of her dressing table mirror as I watched. Looking at herself in the mirror, she would dab little puffs of powder lightly administered to her face until it resembled the fine dust she used to remove when cleaning our furniture. Then standing, wearing her underwear, she would pull a grey skirt over her ample thighs, followed by brown stockings. She would sometimes ask me to brush her hair which I would do nervously as her eyes followed my hand movements. She would then stand, pick up a collared shirt and cardigan, and put on her flat cream shoes, sometimes adding to the ritual with a splash of perfume. My mother never appeared to wear lipstick and later I wondered whether this was due to Daddy's words that, 'No mother of my children will ever straighten her hair or wear lipstick,' to which Mummy would never respond. The finishing touches were when Mummy would open a drawer and pull out a multi-coloured headscarf and a brown handbag which had a shiny clip. I always enjoyed the sound of the clip whenever Mummy asked me to retrieve something from it for her.

All the adults had their large winter coats hanging in the corridor of the house and Mummy would put her coat on just before we walked out, heading for the park.

We would turn left and into another road where the school my cousins attended, St John's, was located on the corner. We'd then cross the road and pass a row of shops – a newsagent, butcher and general store.

As I held Mummy's hand tightly I could see a dark building to my left which Mummy said was a pub called 'The Black Prince' and behind it a brick wall with glass and wire along the top that Mummy explained enclosed a cemetery.

During weekdays there was usually no one around and only occasionally a car or bus. The park appeared forlorn on a bitterly cold winter's day. What few trees there were in the park were bare of leaves, which had fallen onto the asphalt below.

The park consisted of a chain swing with a wooden seat, a metal slide with steps attached and a circular roundabout that was a wooden casing divided into six seats separated by metal bars. It was similar to the one Mummy and I saw on the television show, 'Magic Roundabout'. As we stood in the empty park, watching, I imagined the roundabout spinning to the television show's soundtrack. Mummy's solid arms would lift me onto it and start to push it. Soon I felt I would join the stars of the night sky, my head was spinning so fast.

One spring day, as Mum and I were walking back with shopping bags after visiting local shops, without warning she stopped and rested her bags on the green grass adjacent to an empty paddling pool.

'Look at that,' she said, pointing to a buttercup. What I saw was a tiny resplendent yellow flower, which I hadn't seen before. This felt like an unexplored world miles away from our small room. It felt overwhelming.

Another day she showed me a ghostly looking flower that had lost its bloom so only soft spikes were left – a dandelion. She picked its green stem and blew a hard puff, sending the spikes flying off into the atmosphere. She was introducing me to nature. Mum would also put out crusts of bread on the grey concrete balcony and small birds would come to peck away at their morning feed. I would watch her as she spoke, or sometimes sang, to a fortunate bird. To my hearing they shared a kind of bird language – they understood each other. *I wonder if this can be me one day?* I thought.

Although Mummy had told me we lived in Torbay Road, Kilburn, this information meant nothing to me. I had no idea where we were. I knew Daddy – and in later years, Mummy – would leave the house during the early hours of the morning and return late at night. This was also the case with my uncle and aunt. My cousins I rarely saw because they were older than me and our lives seemed to have no common thread for us to share time together.

I had a taste for exploration but this was frustrated from an early age as there were no-go areas in the house and boundaries that could never be transgressed without fear of punishment. I knew our room was our domain and I explored every inch of it fearlessly. I would touch Daddy's books, opening the pages to try to read the contents, but the big words defeated me. I would gently prise open the wardrobe that contained my parents' clothes and pull them towards me, wondering when they would next wear them. One day I pulled out the tightly tucked bed linen on the queen-sized double bed that we all shared, quickly looking over my shoulder as if I'd carried out an act of vandalism against Mummy's bed-making. Even as I desperately tried to return it to its neat state, I sensed that her invisible presence was already closing in on me. I reproached myself. I was sure to get into trouble, I thought, as I hastily turned down the bed cover. I continued with my exploration despite my fear of discovery and the punishment that might follow. I bent down and poked my head into the dark recesses under the bed and my nostrils picked up the smell of cold and damp. This was where we put our shoes and house slippers. No wonder that in winter when I slipped my feet into them it felt like entering an icy pool, my toes one by one losing feeling until they were like frozen ice cubes. I went over to the window overlooking the garden, where I had only restricted access to use the toilet when Mummy hung out our washing. That was one of Auntie's iron rules, which Mummy did not agree with. But it was not our house to do with as we pleased.

The bottom pane of glass on the right hand side of the window frame was broken and a sheet of newspaper, screwed into a ball and aged by exposure to light and damp, had been stuffed into the gaping hole. I would hear Mummy imploring Daddy to, 'Ask Carmen to fix the damage. What are we paying rent for?' which would be met with silence from Daddy. Then in a frustrated voice, Mummy would express her lack of power with, 'You're a damn fool, Clifford Roach.' I heard no reply, knowing instinctively that overt signs of anger were pointless where my aunt was concerned.

The room was always cold during winter so my home clothing consisted of thick jumpers, T-shirts, and slippers worn with socks. That's how I was expected to cope with the cold. There was an old fireplace in the room and Mum said it used to burn coal to keep the room warm. But we never had coal because the chimney was blocked, Dad said.

The rest of the house was another world from my family's bedroom and I took care whenever I left the haven of our single room. The kitchen contained a large dining table covered with a lace cloth, a large fridge and a display cabinet with plates and cutlery, with a recessed area for a cold food store. Auntie and Mum took turns to cook, with Auntie sharing the gas cooker at mealtimes. The floor was covered with a material called linoleum, or lino, while the rest of the house had wooden floor boards, with the stairs covered by carpet. On the upper floor there were three bedrooms shared between Auntie and Uncle and my four cousins, Cyprian, Stafford, Glen and Charles. The whole house seemed to have what Mum called an 'old' smell, which we readily picked up on our clothes.

The front room was a cornucopia of delights for me. A small television covered by a cloth stood in front of a semi-circle of comfortable chairs assigned to the older members of the family. A large display cabinet contained Auntie's crockery brought out on special occasions. Mum had expensive crockery as well but it was packed in boxes in our room. Then there was a drinks cabinet that Uncle was in charge of and a selection of vinyl records for use on the piece of furniture that consistently fascinated me, a gramophone player. I would open it ever so slowly to peer inside. It had a strange smell and, bending down, I would touch the round vinyl records' grooves as they shone in the light. Hearing voices, I would hastily put the records away in what I hoped was the correct order, then sit down quickly away from the scene of the crime. I would look as if nothing had occurred and up to a point that was true, and I'd wonder what would happen to me if I did get caught as I feared the embarrassment it would cause Mum. I learnt to become invisible at any time during the day and lived to-the-full the adage that, 'Children should be seen and not heard'. So long as I kept out of the adults' way then nothing untoward would happen to me.

'Don't touch this or that,' was the watchword. I would cast a glance over my shoulder to see who was nearby in case I was caught doing something that I shouldn't.

Meanwhile, I was learning to read in the English language at home in our bedroom. Mummy taught me to make sounds from the letters over and over again. She had a quiet, emphatic insistence in saying, 'Now repeat after me,' so that I would copy her 'A, B, C' even though I did not understand. At first my thoughts would wander, and it was if she knew, her voice rising with a slightly menacing tone. She never adjusted her approach or asked me what I wanted. We went through the same sorry experience with numbers. I prayed she wouldn't try to get to a hundred, knowing that '10' was my limit. Fearing the consequences of not remembering, one day I started to cry. Mummy stood up and shouted the numbers, which meant they were now impossible to complete and then she left the room and returned with a wooden rolling pin for rolling out pastry, and to my shock, she attempted to beat me on my head. In a crouching position, I covered my head with my small hands and shouted but not very loudly, 'Mummy, no, please don't.' As quickly as the melodramatic scene had begun, it was over. I slowly uncurled my body and Mummy was standing, the rolling pin still in her hand, repeating, 'I'm sorry!' The violence was over and I'm sure we both longed for it never to occur again. And it didn't. If conflict ever did arise I would become mute or cry.

Most of my memories of my mother are quite the opposite. In the afternoons we would go to the front room and turn on the small screen television. From the corner of my eyes I could see an Aladdin's Cave of family portraits, paintings with flowers, and heavy maroon draped curtains which had a smoky smell as both my auntie and uncle smoked, although I didn't understand what caused the curtains' smell when I was young. It felt so cosy alone with Mum sitting on the floor watching television. Mum would leave the door ajar, listening for activity in the house, hyper-vigilant in trying to avoid trouble. On the TV, a woman's voice would hum a tune: 'Baa, Baa, black sheep, have you any wool? Yes sir, yes sir, three bags full.' Mum and I would sing over the top of the kindly voice of the woman who seemed as if she'd wandered into the wrong job. I thought she should have been keeping home somewhere but definitely not in Kilburn, she was too classy for that. 'And one for the little boy who lived down the lane.' And then a note would sound and the woman with the kindly voice would say, 'Welcome to *The Magic Roundabout.*' Mum and I would follow the sounds of the characters as they counted out numbers and sounded letters to spell words.

On a Saturday morning I would hear the 'rag and bone man'. 'Any old iron?' he'd call and I would run to Mum, asking her to let me outdoors because I didn't want to miss him. He looked so old he seemed to be dead! But he kept repeating, 'Any old iron?' with his cart full of old junk, as he led a grey horse with massive hooves and a mane of hair hanging down over his neck. Both of the horse's eyes were covered and I could hear the metal-shod hooves resounding on the cobbled stone street. I now realise the man resembled a Charles Dickens figure, perched on his rickety wooden bench – as if stumbling from the past with no future ahead. He fascinated me. We would leave out some goods for him. Auntie usually had a throw-out to give him and she'd call out, 'Here you are!' He never spoke up, but mumbled. I was not allowed to talk to him. Mum began to explain in a kindly way, 'He's ...' but Auntie was dismissive. I wondered where he lived and why he did what he did. I was also concerned about how long he lived because after a while he disappeared. I wondered, *Where did he go?*

What I learnt of the world at large was that there were two main activities: education and entertainment. I would think about how one day I'd grow up and I could leave the boredom of our small room in a house dominated by rules and rule-makers.

Chapter 3
Rituals and power

In our family, good manners were inextricably linked with authority.

Trinidadian adults seemed keen to spell out the worst that could happen to me, as I said nothing. I did as I was told and blood curdling descriptions were liberally shared with me, with no thought of the consequences for what was my obviously sensitive nature. I could fall into fear or self-hatred in an instant if directly or indirectly referred to by adults.

Good manners appeared to go hand in hand with 'Good morning's and 'Good afternoon's. As well as 'Yes, Auntie' and 'No, Uncle.' And letting people pass in front of you when out and about. Mum's favourite intonement was, 'Speak when you're spoken to!'

If this sounds vaguely Victorian or Edwardian you'd be right, as it was passed down through the family from my grandparents who were born in the British colony of Trinidad and Tobago in the late 19th and early 20th centuries. Dad was always keen to point out that, 'There was no radio or television back then so you just had to amuse yourself.' Being a child was no easy task.

The oft-repeated adage 'Manners maketh the man' did not

stop me from having mischievous thoughts from a very early age. Mum would talk about never asking parents for anything you didn't have already, and being grateful for what you had rather than focusing on what others had and you didn't. And always to say 'please' and 'thank you' when you were offered something.

Mum had mentioned that some of my baby teeth would start to fall out and new stronger teeth would push through my gums. 'When this happens, tell me,' she said, 'because we have to leave the tooth to the Tooth Fairy.' Tooth Fairy? I wondered what that could be. *Was it similar to the fairy that was on the soap powder Mum used for washing?*

One morning when I woke, I felt the inside of my mouth and found that where I'd had a tooth before going to sleep, it was now missing. The empty socket felt sore and I started to panic, feeling around my mouth for the missing tooth. Maybe I had swallowed it while I slept? Perhaps it was safely secreted in a cavity in my mouth, ready for the Tooth Fairy. Then I saw a spot of blood on my pillow case, and felt a small rough object under the pillow, pulling it out to see the white missing tooth. I jumped out of bed to await Mum's return and when she arrived I showed her my precious tooth. She took it from me and held it in the palm of her hand then placed it in a tissue saying, 'We'll put this under your pillow tonight and in exchange the Tooth Fairy will leave you a five-edged coin, a tuppence, for when you wake up next morning. But you must make a wish.' I wondered what a wish was and why only for a tooth. It sounded far-fetched to me. *But Mummy wouldn't lie, would she?*

That night, Mummy picked up a book of fairy tales which had colour pictures and sat with me on the edge of the bed to read it. 'Once there was a princess who lived in a castle on a hill and she wanted to inherit the kingdom, but for that you had to make a wish, her father said. Yes, a wish. And you had to do it on a loose baby tooth. The princess went to sleep knowing her wish.'

Mum closed the book and began the usual routine of preparing me for bed. This was before the arrival of a nanny who used to look after me when Mummy was busy. Mummy opened her purse and took out some coins, and leaving the door ajar which meant I could see what she was doing, she put the coins into a brown metal box which she called the gas meter. There was some noise and a flame appeared. With that, we both went to the bathroom upstairs for me to wash myself with a blue flannel.

When I woke the next morning, I looked at my pillow to see whether any other teeth had dislodged from my mouth. They hadn't. Simultaneously, I felt under my pillow case and there I felt a coin. Then I realised I hadn't made a wish! I kept that as a secret and, excited, showed Mummy the faded tuppence coin. 'We'll put that away for you,' she said, opening a drawer on her dressing table and popping the money in a box. It was then I decided that even though I hadn't made a wish, that was okay.

Not many days after this first ritual came another that would persist for many years: the cutting of my hair.

'Boy, hold still!' my father bellows.

My hair hits the floor and I look down and see my long, black plaited hair lying in a sad heap on the floor. This is my first cutting of hair and, long before associating it with the Bible's Samson and Delilah, it has made me feel powerless. Dad works his way around my skull as I sit with a white towel tucked in tight about my neck. Dad has tied a knot and I feel his substantial finger pull the knot tight. I don't like it but say nothing.

'Keep still!' he commands, and I do, even though I soon start to play with my fingers and examine the room as Dad snip, snip snips away with a pair of scissors. *Ouch,* as the blade nips my ear. *Can't Dad see I'm angry?* But I keep my opinions to myself.

'Boy, keep your eyes shut!' I imagine I will always be bald. I hate that idea. But low sounds tell me he is pleased with his handiwork.

'Here!' he says as he thrusts a mirror into my hand. I don't want to look, as I will see what is shameful – my dark skin, and big nose and lips. *I'm a mess! Why, oh why, wasn't I born with a white skin? God must hate us, that's why he allows these terrible things to happen.*

At last the ordeal is over.

'OK, shake the loose hair off in the garden,' Dad tells me. He pulls me toward him, his hands overpowering me. I want to run free but his grasp is insistent, without pity for my sensitivity to my new-born head. He makes quick sweeps with the palm of his hand and then stands back to admire his fine work. I look away. Shyness has crippled me. I don't engage with anyone or anything except silence. I've given up.

Chapter 4
Dad's warnings

During weekends I got to see more of my father than during the week. Not that I spent time doing anything with him, as he seemed to spend a lot of time reading the big books on his desk, his back hunched and seemingly oblivious to his small son looking up at him. Mummy explained that Daddy was studying and should not be interrupted and that when I played, I was to do so silently. Well, that wasn't a problem as I had no one to play with so I invented imaginary friends with conversations to match, as usual.

Yet although I understood what not to do, I didn't understand why. Mum telling me, 'Your father is studying law,' meant nothing to me. I wondered where he worked and why he couldn't spend more time with us, as he would go a couple of evenings a week to an unfamiliar place, 'London University', to study law. I felt I hardly saw him. Did that place make him happy, I wondered, when in stolen moments I went into the front room to feel the tomes and make out titles such *Roman Law*. There would be conversations between Mum and Dad about exams, not heated exchanges, and after those talks Dad would leave early in the morning for his work at Maples furniture store on Tottenham Court Road and not get home until very late at night. My brother Fidel and I would see him if he wasn't too late, otherwise we'd be in bed by 7.30 pm and miss him.

But Daddy would sometimes leave that world of books, and studying – and who knows what else, perhaps thoughts of faraway places – to connect with me, awkwardly. That would leave me perplexed.

One Sunday morning, blissfully unaware of the coming information onslaught – and as I was playing on the floor in our room with my toy fire truck and imaginary crew fighting a large fire – Daddy took me and plunged me, at least momentarily, into an adult existence. I heard none of the usual noises that morning from my cousins or even Mummy, who seemed to have been out of our room for a long time. Suddenly, with volcanic swiftness, Daddy announced that I should follow him. When we got to the front room he guided me from behind so both us could gaze at one of my favourite objects there, the cabinet containing all the bottles of drink, which was drunk by the adults and their guests. Daddy said, 'You see this drinks cabinet? You are not to open it or drink anything from the bottles!' He looked at me intensely, which meant I wanted to look away even more.

I knew he had almost finished because he added a declaratory statement with a severe tone. 'You will have plenty of time to drink when you're older.' That was it! With that he stared at the door, indicating I should go ahead of him back to our room, which I meekly did. I had no idea what had given him the idea that the contents of those bottles interested me.

But showing me the bottles of drink and telling me not to open them determined what I would do at the first opportunity. A few weeks later on a quiet afternoon when the only person at home was Auntie, was my opportunity to take a closer look at the amber liquids contained in those bottles. When I saw Auntie busy in the kitchen, I moved swiftly to open the cabinet with a squeak, keeping my ears cocked for the sound of her approach. I paused for a moment, then carried on. Careful only to take the lids off bottles that were already open, I reasoned that there was less chance of detection that way. I put a little liquid into each cap for a tasting. I hated the taste and also realised that if I spilled any or took too much, then the smell might lead to detection. After examining a handful of bottles, I decided not to push my luck, closed the cabinet and returned to our room. Then to my horror, I realised that I may have taken too much from one of the bottles which could lead to my discovery. I decided to add water to the bottle and, with Auntie upstairs, I moved like greased lightning to the kitchen and filled a cup with water. I took the cup to the cabinet, found the offending bottle, filled it, then returned to the kitchen and then our room in short order. I resolved never to do that again.

Some weeks after the drinks cabinet sermon, Daddy was at it again. He spoke to me in the bedroom in what I thought was an earnest tone and, without preamble, launched into a short speech, saying, 'Sometimes you'll see your mother or father naked in the room or house and this is nothing to be ashamed of or worried about, as it's perfectly natural.' Again, that was it! No opportunity for me to question or query his utterance and he immediately left the room, presumably satisfied that he'd effectively rendered a key fatherly duty.

Then in what was the last in the trilogy of 'Thou shall not', one day without warning he said, 'Smoking is not for you,' putting his fingers to his ruby red lips. 'You will have plenty of time to smoke when you're older,' to which I thought, *But why would I smoke?* It's perhaps strange that I had seen my aunt and uncle smoke but it had never occurred to me that this was something I should do. Maybe because neither Dad nor Mum smoked. These subjects were clearly important to Dad but left me confused, again being unable to ask any questions. I responded weakly, 'Yes, Daddy.' Smoking was never mentioned again.

But the warnings didn't stop there. Soon my mother too was harping on about the dangers of a 'den of iniquity.'

I had no idea what a 'Public House' or 'Pub' was – in this case 'The Black Prince'. What mediocre knowledge I had was gained from shopping excursions with Mum on a Saturday afternoon, walking past Mulligan's pub on the corner of Chamberlayne Road and Kilburn High Road, as we crossed at the traffic lights. I would hear the raucous and unfamiliar sound of loud voices and music coming from the upper reaches of the building, and in seconds it drew men towards it, most scurrying back and forth as if they had made a discovery that they were anxious to reacquaint themselves with.

Yet what is expected of me? I wondered. Even if I did have the wit to form a question, there would have been no available evidence to form it. Up until then, I had never seen Mum and Dad so much as sniff any of the coloured secrets contained in the bottles in the glass cabinet of the front room. Indeed, I remembered Dad's forceful words from years gone by, so imagine my shock when out on an excursion with Mum, we made a route change and crossed over the road well before we got to Mulligan's. It was a moving *tour du force*, with Mum stopping for a fraction of time and explaining the dark deeds that took place beyond the darkened doors marked 'SNUG BAR' at the back of the pub. I must never step foot in such a place, she said, and then we were gone, my hand in hers as I surreptitiously wondered what a 'SNUG BAR' was. Maybe we could have one in our room, I thought, as we entered the furore that was Kilburn High Road.

Mum would go out of her way to emphasise how far we were from redemption by talking to me outside 'The Black Prince' Public House on Chamberlayne Road, Kilburn, urging me to promise never to step across what I noticed were intricately tiled steps. As she pulled me away from that den of iniquity, she would talk about how anyone who knew us might see us. But with a quick backward glance, I found the dark glowering interior of the pub strangely alluring.

Chapter 5
English weather and the two bar heater

You couldn't begin to win the war against the English weather without your paraffin canister, used to tackle serious cold in a house where insulation had never been introduced. All of us endured this cruel cold, regardless of age. The living room at night was the warmest room where the body heat generated from the nine of us filled up some of the warmth deficit.

In our room, the two bar heater was all we could rely on, plus the newspaper screwed up to fill the hole in the glass window pane. How the coldness of the room contributed to Dad's chest complaint, I can only speculate.

When I saw the steel grey two bar heater plugged in and glowing, it told me that it was at its maximum power, yet the room still felt cold and smelled of damp, as if the heater had been swallowed and a trick was being played. I would edge closer to it, pushing my toy truck across the thin carpet towards its heat, not wanting to annoy Mummy with noise anywhere else in the house.

One night as I approached the heater, Daddy was sitting upright in a brown wooden chair, his long legs extended outward, so I moved my head to almost touch the chair, with the heater close, directly under his legs. I did not want to wake him for he looked and sounded very tired. I didn't remember having seen him like this before, so my heart went out to him as I continued to play with my truck, making little noises, *vroom, vroom*, pushing the truck backwards with no particular destination in mind. The other thought I had was centred on the feel of the heat from the two heater bars, as I remembered Mummy's frown:

'You are not to go near the heater frame under any circumstances, do you understand?'

'Yes Mummy.'

Then, without warning, I moved my hand towards the red glow of the heater, squirming to get this particular lesson out of my mind. I left the truck game, convinced that Daddy was sleeping, though his eyes seemed open to me, and extended my hand to the delicious red flame. A slight noise at the door alerted me to Mummy or Auntie so I instantly withdrew my hand and looked up to see Mummy's familiar figure standing over me. I would leave getting close to the heater for another day.

But I found it hard to breathe in that cold harsh climate. I needed to flourish in the cold and unforgiving English seasons, but how?

The English were always talking about the weather; Dad and Mum did too. 'Who are these English?' Dad would ask Mum. 'How do they cope with this weather?'

I was perplexed. Were we English or were we some breed apart? Well, we didn't look like the butcher or the man who ran the newsagent. Despite this, they were always talking about the weather as well, so did that make them English? I never got to ask the question but weather was always a topic on par with food or politics. I couldn't keep up with these ideas.

If I was fortunate to leave the house under the protective

custody of Mum (as I rarely went out with Dad), she would sometimes lick her index finger and hold it up to gauge the weather. It was, and probably remains, true that you could have several weathers in the same morning and there were many English words and expressions to match the ambivalence – such as 'drizzle', which was a fine light sprinkling of rain, or 'as light as a feather,' which was one of Mum's sayings. Mum and Dad would say the cold would get into 'the very marrow of your bones,' and that there was 'no hiding place' from the cold blasts. Freezing air seemed to have been manufactured to cause the maximum of tears.

Snow settled on surfaces and would be so high I would be all togged up and excited, both from fear of being swallowed up by this white fairy floss, and just not knowing where to start to walk. Then there was slush which was what snow melted down to.

Whatever the condition of the snow, you had to be dressed warm for that weather, as Mum would fuss over my clothing, then take my hand as we left the house, and say, 'Here we go!'

I felt self-conscious and was stifling under the weight of a thick scarf and wellington boots – that I came to understand should have remained back in the time of the Duke of Wellington. I never successfully managed to put on a pair without rolling on the ground in my attempts. I had a mackintosh for wet weather and a heavy winter coat for winter weather, which was most of the year it seemed to me.

Mum's face would darken as her lips moved and I listened to the flow of her words: 'The English weather,' she would say, 'the English weather is not a thing to be messed with'. She bore down on me with determination so that I would understand that you must always dress for the weather. Aged just three, I could read and spell a little but was not yet ready for school, yet I was already being dressed in an English winter uniform. I had my mittens, and my thick woolly hat would be pulled down almost over my eyes while the rest of my face was left bare. I instinctively hated my scarf as it seemed to choke me, so I was forever tugging it loose to breathe more easily.

Mum, ever vigilant for lapses, would spin me around as she tightened the noose, saying, 'Boy, you'll catch your death of cold.' I had no idea what she was talking about but I obeyed, as in most instances Dad would say, 'You can disrespect me but never your mother,' and raising his hands towards the sky, he'd exclaim, 'She's on a pedestal!' I could see Mum and Dad but no pedestal. *Parents have funny ways*, I thought.

But there was no protection against the fog, which threw its ghostly blanket over you and entered every crack or crevice of your body, so that on returning home I often ran my index finger over my skin to see the result as black soot. Fog would come without warning and you'd be unable to see more than a few inches ahead. You couldn't see anyone else until a bowler-hatted man, usually in dark clothing, was virtually walking on your head. The best remedy as far as Mum was concerned was to stay indoors.

Daily, the weather would preoccupy us, with emphasis on which clothes to wear, and being ready to go out, how to keep warm in fog or rain, and what to wear once you were indoors again. Mum would say, 'We go out in rain, hail or sunshine.' Yet every day seemed so slow due to our methods of coping with the weather. In any season, the day might open with a wintry grimace.

The four seasons – autumn, winter, spring and summer – were evident in the foliage of trees, turning from green to yellow to flame gold, then dropping their leaves at the first hint of winter. I learnt to love autumn and, finally, even winter.

In springtime the snow would retreat to a faded frost. Ice turned into a memory and our clothes became lighter to wear. Our bedsheets would then change from heavy linen to cotton, bringing freshly laundered smells.

The damned weather, that's all the English talked about. Mum would smile; I was bewildered. This presumably was the reason for dressing as if the end of the world might occur at any time in a London hailstorm or snowfall.

All natural light had usually gone from the sky by about 3 pm during the winter months but, even so, it was customary on Sundays to visit family or friends. One afternoon Dad and I had been to some nameless part of London on a visit and were on our way back home. Dad made it clear that snow was not an excuse to not go out.

We would stand at a bus stop waiting and waiting for a red Routemaster bus, which had engines that growled like I imagined a lion would out in the jungle. There I was, stamping my feet to stay warm, wearing a hat and an ever-tightening scarf. I saw nothing on the road, no cars or people. What I had early in my life come to understand was called 'snow' had stopped falling, and now it was as if London had been made invisible by white ash. The air around me was very dark and would have been pitch black if not for the street lights which seemed to me to hang like shiny moons encased in jackets, placed in the dark sky below the stars peeking through. I could see all around me the sight of white carpet, which covered the ground in thick layers, looking as soft as the big blankets we had on our bed at home. Next to me stood my father, as always seeming to me as tall as the trees bare of leaves in this part of London's winter gloom.

Another day I was woken by light piercing the drawn curtains. I breathed in the air with cautious gulps, taking in the lingering aromas of my parents' room. I sat up in my pyjamas and immediately felt cold. When I breathed the air, I could see wisps of my breath escape.

The day before Mum had told me, 'We put the heavy blanket on the bed only when the weather is cold.' And I'd helped her cover the whole expanse of the bed with it, right down the sides to touch the floor. When in that bed, I always felt a sense of warmth and safety under the duvet, wrapping myself tight in the white sheets – with my parents only a breath away. I often heard Dad snoring heavily and even Mummy as well, before drifting off to sleep. I had little understanding of what existed beyond that room and our house. I knew there were buses and cars – those physical things – but did not understand what my part or role was in the wider world except to accept being delivered to a childminder by Mum or to pay a visit to a family friend with my parents. I spent some considerable time contemplating these matters.

I was six and knew that Mum would be calling me to get up and ready for the day ahead. I just wanted to linger in the warmth of bed, drinking in my parents' scent and quickly smelling under my own armpits to see whether the tell-tale smell of fuzzy armpits meant that a bath would be ordered. It was not enjoyable bathing in winter. *Adults should ban it*, I thought. I hated the sound of running the water while trying not to 'freeze to death'. So I took the opportunity to remain in this warm oasis called 'BED', pulling the heavy woollen winter blanket over my head until I felt smothered by my own warmth. I thought about playing cowboys and Indians – until I heard my mother's voice cut through my thoughts with a jolt.

'Wilfred, when are you getting up, boy?'

I dragged the blanket off with one hand and used the other to extricate myself from the sheets, then my feet hit the thread-bare carpet, giving me a start from the freezing cold. My day had started and I was not happy.

Chapter 6
A jam jar

At times I would feel the confinement of living with relatives sorely. I knew to hold my tongue and not give away secrets, and to keep my questions to myself even in the midst of many mysteries that might be hinted at but never fully explained.

One of those mysteries was about a nameless baby boy.

My parents would often talk in front of me as if I were not there. They had early on introduced the twin code: 'Spare the rod and spoil the child' and 'Children should be seen and not heard'. So, yes, my parents saw me but felt no need to hear from me. I was not to get involved in matters that did not concern me, I understood that. The flipside was that I came by a lot of information that I did not understand and I have to would wait years to find out the answers. As a child, I simply coped as much as possible.

'Clifford, if it wasn't for you I would never have lost the baby,' my mother whispered, but with force. She was trying to keep her voice low, because Auntie was on the alert. Dad was seated in our room at a small table with far too many books for it to hold. He sat upright and just seemed to absorb the blows from her words.

What baby? I thought. Knowing not to ask, I carried on

playing on the floor, but stayed acutely tuned in to this rare moment of discord between my parents. Whenever I saw them together there always seemed to be an agreement between them not to argue, even though I could often feel Mum's pent up frustration. But at what or who, I would wonder. They did not want to 'air their dirty linen in public', was the understanding I came to as I grew older. And I would never learn anything more about my mother's miscarriage until I was an adult.

I knew my job was to not cause my mother any heartache and to have her feel proud of me. But that wasn't easy given Auntie's attitude. I came to believe that there was no doubt that living with your extended family would not extend your chances of a happy life.

My aunt was formidable – not in the sense of being amazing but in that, to my tender ears, she never sounded nor appeared happy. She gave meaning to the expression, 'She who must be obeyed'. Except Mummy never got that memo, or if she did she chose not to read it. There was a constant struggle during the years we all lived not-so-happily under one roof. Always a sense that the next argument between Mum and Auntie was only a word away. These women appeared to me to be on a war footing and I would be thinking that I had to do everything possible not to create any further difficulties for Mummy. I usually failed and did not understand why.

Dad and Uncle seemed to have respective household tasks and I never heard them argue or disagree about anything of an evening and at weekends. But that wasn't the case with Mummy and Auntie.

One morning I heard Mummy's firm but insistent tone as I stood next to our partially open bedroom door. She was with Auntie. I could feel a chill breeze float into the room as I stood listening for further signs of trouble.

'Wilfred, can you come here, please?' my mother called out to me.

The gathering storm outside meant I feared I needed the safe haven of our small bedroom, but I walked down the corridor to the kitchen and there stood Mum. There was definitely no smile on her face, while Auntie had the look on her face of someone who was about to be vindicated in something serious, which my stomach was telling me involved me. As Auntie looked on, Mummy, without warning, opened the fridge door and showed me an empty jam jar. 'Did you put water in this?' she asked. I was bewildered about why Mummy would think I would do something so stupid. I knew I wasn't supposed to touch anything of Auntie's even though I might be tempted. I knew I would be caught.

'No, Mummy,' I said, about to cry. Auntie's expression did not change, but her eyes were accusing me of *something*. I could only hope Mummy believed me. *Does she?* I thought. I stood watching these two women staring at each other.

'Carmen, I told you, my son doesn't tell lies.' Mummy's voice was rising in pitch and volume so I knew she was angry at Auntie.

'Alright, alright,' Auntie said, not looking at me. 'I have to go out now.' And with that she was gone.

Mum's use of the word 'my son' seemed to give this whole incident a seriousness that had me confused. Mum sniffed and said it must have been someone else. Her tone suggested she knew who the real culprit was. With that, Mum said, 'Come on, we're going out now too.'

Later that day after Dad had come home, Mum entered our room while I was playing on the floor and told him about what had occurred with Auntie. Dad stood there, still, and I did not hear any reply from him. Mum continued with her denunciation of Auntie and everything she did. Again, Dad did not respond which seemed to make Mum even angrier. I pretended not to hear what was said until Dad replied firmly, 'Shirley, that's enough! You know what Carmen's like,' to which Mum tutted her lips. We all left the room, walking into the kitchen together in what was known as an 'atmosphere' – a tense situation for which I was to blame, though I was thinking all the while that I hadn't put water in the jam jar.

Sometime later, I heard Auntie call out to Mum who was sewing a dress in our room where I was helping her. No one else was at home. Mum and I walked to the kitchen and I saw Auntie with a scowl on her face, standing in front of the fridge. *This is to do with the jam jar again*, I immediately thought. Auntie spoke rapidly, saying that it was Charles who had put the water in the jam jar. But she didn't say that it wasn't Wilfred. I was learning to pay attention to what adults didn't say as well as what they did say.

'Shirley, he's going to get a good beating from his father.'

I kept my eyes looking down at the floor. Mummy replied, 'Well, Carmen, I told you Wilfred doesn't lie.'

There was a moment's silence between the two women. In that moment, I felt shame that seemed to last forever. Shame – with blood rushing to my face. I just wanted to get away, but knew I had to stay by Mummy's side.

With that she broke the silence. 'Come, Wilfred.' And with a quick march we left the kitchen.

Chapter 7
Visitors and culinary challenges

When the doorbell rang making a sharp noise, or when some-one would vigorously knock on the door, in an instant I'd feel terrified. As soon as someone's finger would touch that bell I would leave what I was doing and patiently stand still next to our open bedroom door near the front of the house, waiting for morsels of information from worlds I did not know existed. I would be both excited and worried.

'Hello, Carmen,' a male voice would boom.

'Come in,' would be my aunt's welcoming words. 'How you going?'

'Can't complain. Jesus that cold wind is enough to saw you in two.'

Then footsteps would sound down the hall to the kitchen and as the male voice faded I would slip out of our room, tak-ing the risk of being spotted in order to get a better view of Nat, my uncle's friend who had come to see him. The silence of our room still makes its impression on me.

I would ease my way behind Mum and walk (not run be-cause my mother's words, 'Walk, do not run,' would echo in my mind) heading back the short distance to our bedroom door. I only slightly closed the brown door behind me so that

Mum could see me without announcing her arrival. She had told me, 'Do not close that door unless we are sleeping,' so I would keep the door open. I heard so many whispered conversations from visitors wearing exotic clothes and women smelling of 'fragrance'. I sometimes listened, not understanding what was said in such conspiratorial tones that I heard wafting along from the dining room. Maybe Mum was listening too but I never knew.

One time when Mummy was out, there was a female voice at the front door, one I'd heard before. Then the doorbell rang another four times despite the fact that most people who used it knew that to ring more than once invited Auntie's wrath. I was tempted to run out and ask, 'Who is it?' but I knew Auntie would not want a display of bad manners. I picked up my toy car and crept quietly into the kitchen and under the table set for afternoon tea. Most of the time at home during the week Auntie's caring for me involved her leaving me to my own devices. I did not know these women she had invited around for afternoon tea but I was impressed by their magnificent clothes and the stiletto shoes they wore, and the perfume, oh the perfume, made me excited. Their spoons would tinkle against Auntie's best china and from my position under the table, the scene seemed heavenly.

Auntie spoke to these women with an easy familiarity as if they'd known each other all their lives. Maybe they had. How would I have known? But my parents had earlier mentioned some of their names in passing, saying Auntie had not said kind words about them. Yet here they were drinking tea and eating cake together. As I played under the large dining room table in the midst of a forest of stiletto heels, watching the stockinged feet and absorbing the aroma of some sweet-smelling perfume, the thought came to me: *Why do adults lie?*

Saturday nights were the times for major gatherings at the house for Uncle and Auntie's friends, particularly for men whose names I barely remembered: Sonny, Nat, and Paul who taught maths to my cousin Cyprian.

'Boy, you want a drink?' Uncle would offer guests drinks from the glass cabinet as I hung around the open door watching the to-and-fro of glass bottles from living room to kitchen, and listening to gales of laughter as the kitchen door was often left open. Then I would find a warm spot in the living room in front of Mummy's legs and settle down to watch a TV show before my 7.30 pm curfew, since Mum never joined these gatherings, preferring to sit in the front room.

Then one afternoon I was home while Auntie was looking after me, which meant I kept out of the way, playing mock battles with my soldiers and creating no problems for Auntie. I was happy to comply as there was the possibility of playing with the paper soldiers in our room. I heard the bell pressed more than once and the greeting,

'Hello, Joan.'

'How are you, Carmen?'

Then four more pairs of footsteps along the hall. Were they similar to the high heels Auntie wore, her stilettos? I'd had a fascination for those shoes ever since first climbing the stairs to put hers out for the day.

So I left my toy soldiers' battle and picked up a small truck, moving down the corridor to see who had arrived. No adult noticed or cared if I was there listening to every word of exchange. I wondered why Auntie seemed so nice to people she obviously didn't like. 'Why do adults lie?' was the question still in my mind. Even though I had no idea what they were talking about, I knew adults had something called 'secrets', not to be told to anyone else – just like the time I heard Mum and Dad arguing over a brother I never knew. These were not child-friendly events.

Living through these visits seemed to me like holding my breath over a period of five years or more. My focus on exhaling seemed to take the rest of my life. I wanted to escape the ritual of being displayed to all the adults with their witticisms: 'Hasn't he grown? Do you know your times table? We can see he'll be a big boy! Look at that head – big brains!' And so it went on. I ached to escape but there was nothing to do but face it. I was fair game.

Sometimes I would hide behind the sofa. I could just about fit in there without being suffocated and my trick was to get there before the adults came into the room, even though it must have been an open secret. I knew they knew I was there but, just in case, I breathed softly. No one bothered me until my curfew hour was pulled back to 7 pm and it was time for our warm dark room and bed. I wanted Mummy – but no sign of her. Dimly aware of time passing, I made up stories in my head. Words from children's songs floated by: 'Two little boys and two little girls,'. And tears would stain my cheeks.

I breathed disappointment to myself on Saturday mornings. 'Not again,' I'd think, anticipating that familiar day and then night routine.

One Saturday morning chore I did look forward to, though, was getting out of the house and down to the shops. Soon I was entering the butcher's shop and looking down at the sawdust that covered a wooden floor sometimes stained with blood. Then to look up and see a row of chickens clearly dead, with their necks elongated and bodies usually plucked of their feathers.

Mr Kaye's butcher shop was around the corner from home, next to the newspaper shop. I knew that I was not allowed to speak or reply to any adults, the exception being Auntie Carmen, Uncle Norman and, of course, Mum and Dad. I had a habit of not looking at anyone's face. So I squinted at Mr Kaye, hoping he hadn't seen me. He always had.

'Hello, young man,' he bellowed, with what seemed to me a dangerous smile. *Does he use that on the birds hanging in the window and lining the wooden counter?* I thought.

I returned a shy quick smile which did not come from my eyes. I noticed the smell of dust mixed with blood then looked up and saw a row of chickens – necks stretched, dead silent, feathers attached. I felt sick. I looked to Mummy for reassurance. She was seeming to take forever to reply to Mr Kaye. At the end of this comforting interlude I remembered Mum's rule, 'Speak when you're spoken to'. *Why does he want to ask me anything? Why can't he ignore me?*

As he continued to beam his unwanted smile like an x-ray from Dr Who, to my relief he turned his attention to Mum, asking, 'How are you, Mrs Roach?'

Mum answered with a smile. 'Just fine, Mr Kaye, just fine,' to ensure there were no further probing questions from him.

As they spoke, I moved the sawdust backwards and forwards with my shoe, slowly and silently. This movement absorbed my worried attention as I knew from previous shopping expeditions with Mum that there was no escaping the hard grip of her hand as she held mine, yet it was also reassuring.

Just when I thought my wish for invisibility was working, she stared down at the top of my head. This was a more worrying signal. In an instant I stopped what I thought was my quiet foot movement.

Frustrated, I didn't dare show it. Any defiance on my part – or as Mum called it, 'rudeness' – could and would be dealt with by a stare if I was lucky, or if not, a slap, and being told in anger how not to behave.

My right hand fitted Mum's left hand like a small walnut, with her fingers short but elegant, curled around it. So it felt safe for me to look up, and the sight that greeted me was, to my innocent eyes, breathtaking. So many birds, some feathered some not, strung up on large metal hooks, their necks stretched to breaking point, as if they would snap if I continued to stare at them. *I hate this place*, I thought.

I could not wait to leave, and looked towards the door.

Mum seemed unaware of my thoughts. This cheered me up no end as she silently gazed at the array of pigs' heads, which were safely, to my relief, propped up behind the glass counter.

Mr Kaye, with a hat on and dressed in what appeared to be a huge white blanket, stood as if to attention on a parade ground, while Mum inspected the severed pigs' heads. As Mr Kaye waited for Mum's decision, I wondered, *What has happened to the rest of the pig?* I would soon find out as Mum selected several cuts of meat.

Meanwhile the heads hung there, their dead dead eyes looking straight back at me, so I was fearful that the heads could see me. To me, the smell was like a room at home just after you wake up.

On returning home, it was always the same routine., Mum would singe off the feathers that remained on the chickens, as well as remove the pigs' guts, while I watched on. 'You can't leave this in the meat and cook it or you'll get sick,' she'd tell me. Then she'd put the carcass in a large dish, adding salt, pepper and garnishing, with onion and garlic. If Auntie was around they'd have a chat about how good the meat was and the weaknesses of English culinary habits. Then the finished carcass would go into the fridge overnight, ready for Sunday roast dinner.

I would breathe in the disappointment of having to wait, and I'd think, *Not again*. It was the familiar routine on a Saturday morning.

But there was some compensation for me. After visits to the butcher, once home there would always be the contents of the bags spilled onto the kitchen table and Mum and Auntie poring over the various bits of bloodied pig meat. In unison they'd say, 'That's a good cut,' or, 'Yes, a nice man' – the kind of discussion which was a rare ceasefire in hostilities. They'd divide the meat between them and put the chunks of flesh offcuts, such as pigs' snouts and trotters, into large glass jars, adding water, herbs and lemon. I never knew when the sous would be ready to eat but on a random Saturday, Mum would call from the kitchen, 'Come, boy, and eat some sous,' and I would head for the feast, together with the adults and my cousins. This seemed to be one project where there was no overt hostility between Auntie and Mum.

At first Mum made reassuring noises to me about how I'd enjoy the sous. Although initially my tastebuds were suspicious, I soon grew to like it, biting into the fleshy parts of the pig chunks, with bristles still attached, which had at first alarmed me.

'Eat up boy!' It was a communal coming together of the two families and, to my shock, everyone was laughing away as the juices dribbled down our chins.

Sous was only eaten on Saturday morning, with fish eaten on a Friday and meat on a Sunday – all very biblical.

Chapter 8
Prayers to Jesus and home routines

Come winter, the arrival of snow meant it was my job to take Dad's slippers out from under the bed and have them ready to put on his feet when he got home from work. I would then put his Oxford brogues back under the bed, still shining since morning. As I grew older I would have to shine them, exerting myself to within in an inch of my life on Sunday afternoons.

It would appear on the face of it that Mum and Dad had agreed to leave my prayers to God as it was one of the tasks Dad would take responsibility for, so it would be largely left undone.

'Wilfred, it's time for bed!'

'Yes, Daddy.'

Always Dad, never Mum, took me to say a prayer out loud, and I was never quite sure who this man Jesus was. On our hard wooden floor in a room lit only by moonlight or table lamp, I would obediently get down on my knees to pray, trying to get comfortable but couldn't.

'Gentle Jesus meek and mild …' the words stuck in my throat, 'Look upon this little child. Pity my simplicity …' Pity me because I couldn't remember much more of the prayer.

Dad had told me about Jesus but I didn't understand what

he'd said.

Fear of the dark consumed me. *What is that in the corner?* I didn't know. The tall and usually silent figure of my father was now asking me in low tones to repeat what I could not remember. 'Repeat after me,' he'd say. I did try.

The church-going was pursued by Mummy, not Dad. I had never been to a church until one day she said we were going to attend a service. I was uncertain and thought it best to say as little as possible. On a cold afternoon, Mum and I walked to a building that did not impress me, a sort of muddy brick red colour. We entered through large wooden doors and came upon burning candles that created a scene I couldn't cope with, so I immediately wanted to leave. Mum had said something about St Michael but I didn't understand what a church was or what you should do there. So when a man with a large belly approached us, I felt a fear which lessened only when I realised there were other children in the building.

Every night after my prayer ritual, when our room was so often cold, Mummy would make a cup of Milo milk, and then came the joy of getting into bed. By this time I was sharing my parents' bed and everybody had their station: Mum lay in the middle, I would lie beside her facing the wall and Dad would lie on the garden window side of the bed.

'You mustn't switch on the light,' Mum would say, showing me. But I really had no interest. Then when I woke in the night, needing to use the toilet, I was confused but didn't want to cause upset. *Ooh, my stomach!* I imagined hobgoblins like on television, such as Dr Who's Daleks, screaming, 'Exterminate, exterminate,' and pursuing me down a dark corridor to the outside toilet. I looked around the darkened room and knew I had to face the dark because my need to urinate was urgent!

Pulling the bedcovers aside, I felt the cold of our room, shuffled my feet and found my slippers, then with my night eyes, as mummy referred to them, I saw the white door knob and left my sanctuary for the unknown. I felt my way along the wall, cold to the touch, what was a short distance but seemed miles to me, creeping along the corridor. I stopped at the one step drop, the cellar door on my right, then trying not to walk into the huge dining table that resembled a space ship, I looked over my shoulder, sensing demons or such like within the sleeping household. I felt bitter resentment at having to use the outside toilet. A blast of cold air, the darkness shrouding the flowers to give them a ghostly outline, then knowing my fear was just beyond the wooden door, I pulled at the old handle. Now I wanted it to be over fast! I rushed in pulled my pyjamas bottoms down a little and heard the reassuring sound of pee, which meant I wasn't completely alone. I stopped peeing, and not wanting to cause a fuss, yanked the chain, heard a flush, rushed out and back, then to my horror, I thought the door was locked. Stuck out in the cold, I knew I would have to go around to the garden window and alert my parents. But the door was open after all, and I retraced my steps without incident, climbing back into the warm bed which my parents had not stirred from. I turned and faced the wall, and soon fell asleep. What an ordeal it had been!

At home I was often on my own, which didn't bother me too much at first as I knew nothing else. My first cousins were there but effectively I had no relationship with them apart from seeing them at meal times, or when we gathered around the television. Three of four of the boys had been born in the 1950s and only the last was close to me in age.

So, mostly alone at home, I would play with my toy soldiers. *Bang, Bang, Whoosh*, as I'd make the cannon blow away the opposition soldiers. Sometimes, as a 'King' or 'General' on a horse, I commanded my troops to crush the enemy. All the action took place on the floor of our room and I had the privacy of my own world where I could think up the next battle plot. Auntie or Mum never asked me why I did it, and mostly when I asked for paper they would hand me white sheets of paper to draw on and scissors which excited me, though sometimes they refused. As I drew with pencil or crayon, I would imagine the battles these soldiers could fight. I would always be the 'General' or 'King'. My heart would sink if I heard the key in the door earlier than usual in the evening as it was the sign that Dad had come home, and there was never enough time for me to clear away the evidence of battles! The door to our room would open and Dad would stand there surveying the scene.

'Boy, what have I told you about playing with paper?'

Feeling both a sense of obedience and resentment, I would scuttle to put my waste in the bin until the next time. But, inside, I felt as if I was boiling water. At those moments I'd think about how Mum would put the metal pot on the stove, turn the gas on, light a match and place the pot on the metal grill waiting for it to boil. She'd then get the rice out of the container in the cupboard, using her right hand to measure out how much rice she wanted to use. As the water boiled furiously, she added the rice which made a *shush* sound, making me jump.

Dad would return home looking exactly as I remembered him from the morning, with his black lunch satchel, dark coat and dark flat cap.

When I'd hear that key in the lock, I would run to the door and there he'd be, tall against the dark outside with just the street lamp to the illuminate the houses behind. His black bag looked like those that doctors carried.

'Hello Wilfred,' he'd say and touch my head. Mum would come out of our room and then our evening would start. I would have to wait for him to change into his home clothes to perform the grandfather clock ritual. That large clock seemed to take up a lot of space. When I looked at it, I thought it might speak to me.

First, he would have a chat with Mum in the kitchen or our room. Then I would follow him to our room, he'd change, and then from a drawer he'd pull out a long key. We'd walk along to the clock and I would try to see where he put the key. He'd insert it and wind it anti-clockwise several times, then remove the key and wait for the clock to sound at 7 pm. And it always did. We'd then return to our room, he'd put the key away and we'd find out what was for dinner.

Generally, Uncle would come home from work before Dad and I would be waiting at the front door, looking at what he was doing through a crack in the door. He would talk to me and ask me how I was.

Once inside, Uncle pulled the high, heavy curtains closed, checking that the windows were locked. I would stand at a distance while he performed the task then, turning with a smile, he'd bend down and touch my head lightly and in that moment I could smell the scent of cigars on his fingers. I guiltily welcomed his attention as he seemed kind and interested in me in a way my father was not.

Those deep maroon curtains always seemed dusty and grey. I was sure that greyness came from the fog which always left dirt in your nose and on your skin. Once when no one was looking, I had entered the front room to examine them more closely, feeling the soft silkiness and smelling them. *Ugh,* I thought, *they smell old and musty.* So I beat a hasty retreat.

Uncle, being a tall man, seemed to engage in a fight with those drapes, pulling from the left and then right until only a fine chink of streetlight was allowed into the room. He would switch on a table lamp to illuminate the room. That was the signal for my cousins to enter.

Mornings had rituals too. Large coins had to be pumped into the gas meter at what seemed a rate of knots to get enough hot water for bathing or washing clothes. The brown box conveniently sat outside our room and Mum had the unpleasant task of servicing it.

Clink, clink: that was the sound of the heavy coins entering the gas meter box like spare bullets. I was unable to see them as the meter was attached to the wall far above my head. It was early morning and the house would be empty, apart from Mum and me.

'Wait here,' she'd say as she put the coins in. I don't remember how many but I knew it was the difference between cold and tepid cold water.

'Isn't it amazing how we never get the hot water we need,' I'd hear her say as the last coin hit the box, almost as if she were speaking to herself. I would stand mute, watching. 'Wilfred, go upstairs and try the hot water for me.'

'Yes, Mummy, it's hot,' I'd call out.

'OK, you can have a bath. Let me know when you're finished.'

So many inhibiting conditions had an effect on me as I grew. I would speak in my head rather than to adults; I don't think I trusted them at all. Increasingly, I didn't speak. I felt misunderstood and angry but to speak out hadn't worked so I turned to a non-verbal activity, cutting out paper soldiers. I hardly saw Dad except first thing in the morning and then when he returned for the ritual of the clock. Mum was not around a lot of the time, and Auntie, who was nominally looking after me, would sit and smoke without so much as even blowing smoke in my direction. That relative non-attention pleased me as I conjured up my battle scenes and arranged the soldiers on the floor in our room. I would quietly find pieces of unlined white paper to either tear up or use to draw outlines of soldiers, keeping the door part-open so Auntie could see what I was up to. She never entered our room. Did Mum ban her? I felt that was our inner sanctum.

Sometimes I'd climb up to look through the closed French windows – a brief moment of freedom.

'Please don't go in the garden,' my mother would say, her eyes ablaze with worry, while I felt desperate to understand why not. I would press my face up against the window pane, lips cold from touching the glass, and I'd blow air onto the pane, creating a big imperfect circle with my breath.

On a rare occasion I was allowed to step onto that foreign ground, the garden. Once, Mum unlocked the door and I heard a strange noise, unfamiliar to me: children playing together. The sound had travelled from St John's school, five minutes from our house.

Chapter 9
Early days at school

One morning in early September 1966, Mum told me, 'You'll be starting school soon which means you'll learn and be taught by teachers.' That's how I found out that I would become a part of the world outside the door and walls of 40 Torbay Road. I had turned four at the beginning of 1966 and that was the age children went to infants' school, transferring to primary and eventually secondary school at age eleven.

St John's Infant and Primary School was made of many small bricks and looked very old. As I waited with Mum to enter the building, I saw two wooden arches under which were written in huge letters, 'BOYS' and 'GIRLS', carved into the stonework, which seemed greyish and forbidding.

I wanted to stay with her gentleness, her soft voice and motherly bosom that I would lean against. She would protect me but these teachers wouldn't. I came to understand that they could not visualise who they were and how they seemed to me.

I don't think I had any real concept of what school – as education – meant. In my mind it just took me away from my beloved mother to an environment with shrieking and shouting kids. I have no recollection of Mum explaining what 'going to school' was really about, but I do know that on that September morning, dressed and with my hair brushed, I seemed to know that something important was about to occur. I know that I felt uncomfortable and exposed. Did I realise I was already exposed due to the colour of my skin?

I had a school bag that hung from my right shoulder and I walked beside Mum, never running, shouting or doing anything boisterous, in remembering the rules of home: 'Children should be seen and not heard'.

No gloves for me at first but in future they would always be packed, just in case. My hair was short, so no problems there.

On that first day Mum and I walked together through a red painted wooden door. Then Mum stood still for a moment, surveying the tumult of children, laughter and tears.

There were two long queues for the younger children, and I felt my lack of stature. It was the first day of school for me but many other children were returning from summer holidays, with stories of adventures. I was going into the infants' class and could not even speak.

Then Mum was gone and tears and terror filled my eyes and stomach. What was I supposed to do? I looked for friendly faces that I knew and then in an instant saw my cousins! But when they looked at me it was not a welcome look, it was a 'stay away' look as if from complete strangers. I longed for them to come over to me or give me a friendly wave. My shyness prevented me from crossing the invisible barrier that seemed to exist between us on my first day at school. And I never had contact with them at school again.

Initially Mum collected me from school, then she made an arrangement with Vera – Auntie Vera to me – her friend who lived in a house similar to ours with her school-aged daughter, Sandra. It had a very dark corridor and a black dog that I feared. But Auntie Vera was always smiling and I always ate a nice tea there.

After tea, Mum would come from somewhere, I didn't know from where but it must have been work, to pick me up from Vera's. We would walk home without saying much and then I'd change into home clothes and stand at the kitchen table while Mum prepared the evening meal.

I remember my first test at school was a real challenge.

I didn't know how to spell my own name, and learning to count seemed to have frozen since I'd started school. I felt out of shape, unwanted and trapped. How long would this schooling take? Time dragged.

One morning in class my teacher asked me to go with her to see another teacher in what turned out to be an empty room painted white with just a table, chair and filing cabinet in it – no other children. My thoughts were confused. Small blocks of wood of different sizes were scattered around. The teacher explained what I was to do but it made no sense to me and I was too embarrassed to say I didn't understand.

'I will be back soon,' she said as she closed the door behind her.

I stared at the blocks in panic. I moved some blocks to match the others, such as yellows with blues and blues with yellows but it still made no sense so I gave up. I looked around the room, stood up and walked around, then went back to the blocks – and waited. I had to work with the blocks to see what I could make. She'd be back to check on me, I thought, so I have to memorise them. I saw a range of different coloured pinks, reds, greens, similar to Lego. *But this is not play time*, I thought! Alone in the room, I wondered if Mum or Dad would ever find me.

Then the door opened and the blank face of a teacher appeared. Without a touch of feeling, she asked me if I had finished. I looked down shyly and mumbled, 'Yes.'

'You can go,' she said. *I can leave. What does it all mean?* I felt responsible, but for what? For unspoken untruths.

The lingering question was would I get into trouble. No one mentioned the bricks again, not at home or at school.

Chapter 10
Christmas Nativity

I knew Christmas was coming due to my involvement in the Nativity re-enactment at St John's. The teacher had asked, 'Who wants to join the choir?'

I'd scanned the room of shiny-faced children and saw one hand go up, then another, then felt mine go up even though I tried not to draw attention to myself.

'Wilfred, you're in the choir!'

Oh, now I will have to tell Mummy and she'll be angry, was my first thought. But she wasn't. She smiled and said, 'I want to come, and will see if I can come'. I was quietly elated.

The day came. It must be Christmas, I thought, as all the decorations we had helped create – such as the loops of red and green – were on display, the green Christmas trees hung with gaudy balls and a white angel sitting atop.

My school friends and I were gathered at lunch time near St John's school hall as it filled with adults, their eyes peering about while we waited for the signal from our teacher to make our entrance accompanied by music.

To the strains of 'Once in Royal David's city stood a lowly cattle shed, where a mother laid her baby in a manger for his bed,' we began the procession to Jesus's crib at the front of the hall. My first Christmas Nativity – my crown glittered, the bed sheet Mum had given me draped along the floor, and I carried a gift for the baby Jesus. Yet my overriding concern was to see Mum's promised presence. And there she was, tucked among the other mums, all with smiling faces. Now I could complete the performance with no difficulty at all.

Christmas changed the usually incendiary mood of the house to one of jollity: 'Glory to the new born King, Christ's Emmanuel!'

Uncle, with Dad's help, had procured and put up the Christmas fir tree in the front room. I had sneaked in when the adults were busy. Because usually if I was found there I would be asked, 'What are you doing in here?' and I would know from the tone of the adult's question that they assumed I was up to no good. This time I had admired the tree, wondering when it would be decorated.

Auntie blew the dust off the Christmas decorations box, opening it for me to see an assortment of large and small Christmas tree balls.

'Wilfred, hand me them, one at a time,' she said, standing on a step ladder leaned against the tree, and she hung each bauble as I handed it to her. I rummaged through the box of presents, now feeling in charge of preparations in the run-up to Christmas. Auntie had decreed there would be no decorations in the rest of the house, only the front room, as she didn't want any marks left on the walls.

Mum would busy herself with sending Christmas cards and buying presents. 'Would you like to meet Father Christmas?' she asked one day and my reaction was *Who is that?* Mum showed me a leaflet with a man who had white skin and a white beard and hair, wearing red clothes, including a red cape. He looked so unlike Dad he scared me. I said, 'Yes,' to her question because I knew that was what Mum wanted.

Saturday morning Mum and I went to the local Woolworths store for my appointment with Father Christmas. The store was different – full of decorations – and near the entrance was an igloo with a man, who resembled the one in the picture Mum had shown me, sitting beside the igloo. A line of children and mothers seemed excited to meet this old man. Not me. I was hoping it would end as quickly as possible and we could go home.

'Ask Father Christmas if he'll grant your wish,' my mother whispered. *Wish?* I thought, *Mum, why?* Father Christmas asked me to sit on his knee. I was not comfortable with this as I looked into his fake beard, crinkled white skin and red tunic. I couldn't wait to get away.

'Ho, ho. I am Father Christmas.' *Really?* I thought. Mum was standing, not smiling. I wasn't sure why we were going through this ordeal. He patted his hand and asked me again to sit on his knee. He wasn't my father but what could I do? It seemed Mum wanted me to, as she had a look on her face like torture. As I sat there, he leaned into me and my dislike of Father Christmas was cemented as I wondered how I could avoid this old man's breath. But the question was asked, 'What would you like for Christmas?' I was stumped as Mum had always told me never to ask for anything. Then the first thing that came into my head was, 'A fire engine.' As he held me, he reached with his other hand into a large bag and took one out.

On Christmas morning I slid out of bed to be greeted by a cold corridor and no one around. I tip-toed into the living room to see the tree resplendent with baubles, paper rings, and silver balls – but the presents, all garishly wrapped, were what interested me. *How many have my name on*? I wondered. Before I could discover this, Auntie's voice erupted from the kitchen. I'd been caught out snooping.

I sneaked a look at the tree after the Roach's and Clarkes had finished eating and Mum and Auntie had cleared up. It was a hiatus until the Christmas pudding was ready to eat, all aflame with brandy, and cream to follow. Uncle Norman dished up a helping for all and I was told, 'If you are a good boy you might find tuppence in the Christmas pudding'. I wanted to find that round five-edged coin and make a wish. But the wish was secondary. A large dessertspoonful of pudding was plonked into our white earthenware bowls and I was filled with the expectation of success. And then, yes! There it was, but not a tuppence. It was a smaller coin. 'I've found it!' I said, hesitant.

'Let me have a look. Yes, he has,' Mum said, holding it up. 'Lucky he didn't swallow it,' I heard as the adults spoke about me, not to me.

I wanted the attention on me to stop, and to become invisible. Mum handed the coin to me, but I was no longer interested and finished the rest of my pudding in silence. Pudding was followed by tea and Mum's black cake which tasted so good, full of fruit and liquor. Then came the Queen's Speech with the Queen intoning, 'Happy Christmas to you all'. And that was it, a happy Christmas chorused by the snores of the adults and completed with the disappearance of my cousins.

Left to my own devices, I would find some presents, which I had placed in our room. One year I received a spinning top and a car. There was a silence on Christmas afternoon that already resembled the dark of night. I quietly entered our room. There Dad would be sitting upright, asleep on a wooden chair.

I would look at him wondering if my quiet play would wake him. He always appeared to be dead. Yet that thought did not deter me as I would quietly get down on the floor with my knees touching the thin carpet, the cold hitting them like two daggers. I persisted in driving my car around and around with a one bar heater flickering, barely clinging to life or giving off any warmth.

A memory from another Christmas-time meal sets the tone for what a special celebration it was for the family.

'Wilfred, come and eat,' my mother calls. I survey the white table cloth, sigh a little, and wait. Playing with the edges of the cloth I feel the weave, while my body remains perfectly still. Mum carries in the white earthenware bowl with a cover the colour of creamy soap. I smell the rice and peas before the dish is placed on the table, and then on my plate: the pungent smell of gunga peas, resembling brown pellets, so small and with a nutty flavour, and then the smell of cooked spinach.

Dad comes in to take his seat.

Then he looks at the knife and fork on the left of my plate, and on the right, nothing, no spoon for dessert. Mum asks with sincerity, 'Wilfred, what's wrong?' I remain mute, my thoughts wanting me to say, *Mummy, there's no spoon.* But although I purse my lips to speak, no words leave my mouth and I slump a little.

'Oh, I see,' she says, with evident relief.

Her face moves closer to mine, and I can smell the powder she uses for her face, with a little perfume behind each delicate ear. How do I know where the perfume is placed? Well, I have watched her in our room.

So now the missing spoon must be found. Within a moment there it is, sitting in its rightful place, to my right. I smile shyly, wondering whether I should have said something.

Chapter 11
My brother joins our family

One bright weekday in early June, 1966, when I was four, Dad said to me, 'Come on, get yourself ready. We're going to the hospital.' Dad seemed displeased by something as we hustled onto the red bus heading to the hospital. What I knew for certain from the limited information provided by him was that we were going to see my 'baby brother'. I was struck by confusion about what changes this event might bring.

At the hospital we walked up the front steps and stood in front of a lift cage with stairs on either side. The lift was painted black with grill-like lattice openings, similar to Mummy's steak and kidney pie, but large enough to stick your fingers through. Daddy pressed number '5', on a gold-plated board with what seemed to be hundreds of white buttons with black numbers on them. The lift was creaking as if it had a bad cold, slowly grinding its way to the destination Daddy had promised – the ward where Mummy and the new baby were to be found. I just wanted to see Mummy again. It seemed like forever since I'd last seen her. I hadn't seen a real baby except on television and couldn't understand the concept of having a baby brother.

I was worried in the lift, looking up and down but unable see where the ropes began and ended as they disappeared magically into a dark cavernous sky above and also depths below. I would hear footsteps and see the stockinged legs of women, occasional glimpses of an ankle or where a dress ended. I gripped Daddy's hand until the lift finally arrived at its destination and the metal gates opened wide to a sun-filled ward.

Within moments my baby brother, Fidel, had entered my life. And although I don't remember anything more about the hospital visit, I know that soon enough he was the focus of attention for everyone in the family.

He was incorporated into our daily lives, and I learned to feel a responsibility for him. I remember by about the age of about eighteen months he would crawl up the stairs, and I would try to stop him from falling, following him at close quarters.

One particular workday morning, I stood at the bottom of the wooden stairs, which had deep red carpet held in place by metal rods. I looked up and down those stairs with trepidation. I knew I had climbed those stairs as a toddler myself a long time before, one step at a time. And now this small bundle called Fidel, my baby brother, was heading in the same direction. In the mornings, Mum and Auntie would sit in the kitchen, while I looked after Fidel, dressed in my school clothes. They'd watch the clock so I would not be late for school.

One of my new duties was to shepherd my brother safely up the stairs to Auntie's bedroom. By now I knew Fidel's ways well: he had taken my cot, and he constantly ate, gurgled or mouthed words as the adults tried to coax words from him with funny faces and grins. Often I stood feeling helpless, rendered mute but wanting to show how I was helping my brother. In the morning, step by step we'd go up the stairs, and I would guide him with my hands, keeping my eyes glued to his nappy.

The morning sunshine streamed through every crack, crevice and window pane as if to give me enough light for my vital task.

I felt Mummy's guiding presence even though she was in the kitchen. Just a few more steps to the top of the stairs, which had a musty smell that my nostrils fought against. With both eyes carefully following the chubby feet of my baby brother as he took each step up the faded carpeted stairs, I felt disgust seeing clumps of grey dust which had accumulated in the corners, and I would try to avert my eyes.

At the top of the stairs I would move steadily along the corridor with Fidel. Reaching the door to Auntie and Uncle's bedroom, I would hesitate, hearing the sounds of Auntie's and Mummy's voices wafting up the stairs. Then, stepping over the threshold into Auntie and Uncle's bedroom, I detected a scent of perfume and the room having been slept in. I would look at Auntie's dressing table adorned with a powder puff and her jewels, a chair stacked with clothes and their unmade bed.

I had developed an interest in Auntie's clothes. I can't remember when it started but I would go up before Auntie went to work. I'd always been told by Dad not to go in there but I did go in, and chose her stiletto shoes. Then Fidel copied me. Did I encourage it? I'm not sure. But I was certainly right behind his intention to find Auntie's clothes and shoes as he took each step up the threaded carpet. Then he would get out her underwear, including her bra, as I regarded my cleverness in helping him reach his goal safely.

Chapter 12
My parents' bed

My move to the large bed that took up most of our room was due to Fidel's entry into the world, because on his arrival home he was put to sleep in my cot.

So it was all change and I found myself in an unfamiliar environment where I slept on the edge, beside the wall, lying there curious to know what was under the dark hollow of the bed, thinking something lurked down below where my father's slippers were kept.

I was propelled from a caged setting, which was impossible to climb out of, to being on the end of a row of bodies. It wasn't just a new world but a different universe. The only way to keep the bed warm – but not the room – was by placing a hot water bottle between the sheets an hour before bedtime. The hot water bottle was 'filled with water hot enough to scald,' Mum would tell me in a firm voice.

The change in routine was reflected in my bedtime ritual, which I found disagreeable – but what could I do about it?

I would feel a rising sense of panic that I would soon be sent off to bed, so I would try to make myself as still as possible, hoping to avoid my father's unwanted gaze. Then I'd sense the game was up and, sure enough, even though there was no illumination in the room to see the clock showing 7.30 pm, the timing of the television programmes was as regular as a red bus. I knew it was time for bed and soon enough the ominous words would sound out.

'Wilfred it's time for your bed,' Dad would say, at which command I would reluctantly reply, 'Yes Daddy,' then kiss Auntie and Uncle, then Mum and Dad, goodnight.

Leaving the cosy front room, I had to remember not to close the door tight but to leave it ajar. I would stand in the dark corridor and briefly look out through the front door to see the street light shining, as it provided a little light for me to see where I was going. Mum had told me not to switch on the hall light, so in darkness I would make my way to our room. I would switch on the light, collect my toothbrush and towel, switch the light off, and gripping the bannister, carefully thread up the twelve steps to the landing in darkness. Mum's words would echo in my head: 'Wilfred, go upstairs to the bathroom – but you're never to touch any towels or other items belonging to the Clarkes.' On reaching the bathroom and switching on the light, I would quickly brush my teeth and wash my face and hands, dry them, and make a descent to our room as fast as possible, knowing that Dad would shortly enter and expect me to be ready to complete my nightly prayers, under his supervision.

Every week night I was expected by Mum and Dad to be in bed by 7.30 pm, though the rule was relaxed on Saturday night. I could stay up a while longer, joining the adults and my cousins to watch a variety show or a film on the small television in the far corner of the front room. I remember for a period there was another unusual incentive for me to stay up, a young woman who used to visit us some Saturday nights, a cousin's girlfriend, Tia. We never spoke nor did Mum mention her to me – it was as if she were a ghost in our midst. She stood tall with blonde hair and milky white skin. I had not seen a woman with her colour in the house before. She seemed to tower over me, to glow with porcelain beauty like one of Mummy's rare plates. I was curious but wary of talking to her. What could I say? Yet she always encouraged me with a smile or hello. I felt she was special and looked at me with kindness. We would all gather as usual in the front room to watch Dr Who on television. There were nine of us cramped into the lounge room, so there was no place for me to sit. I would find a spot to wedge myself in next to Dad and Uncle, my leg touching Dad's.

One night during the school holidays in August 1969, we sat and watched the moon landing, one of the few times that we were all in the front room, and transfixed by television. I remember how slow the connection took, until the 'one small step for mankind' declaration by Neil Armstrong. I sat alongside Fidel and I marvelled at that grainy transmission that showed us what was happening up on the moon.

The nights in front of the television were generally cosy, but come morning often there might be some difficulty. I might hear Mum say, 'Wilfred, get up. You've wet the bed again.'

Fearful, I would feel the warm wetness and I'd wait, as if in a dream, my tears welling up. Silent, as if in prayer, I'd hope not, then doze to sleep again, before a shaft of light would wake me to the unwelcome sensation, a damp patch near my leg. Then more, as I moved my hand tentatively to find a bigger patch, cold to the touch. Startled, I'd think *This is nothing to do with me.*

Mum would stir; Dad was already up. *Has he noticed the smell that fills my nostrils?* I'd wait for the words from Mummy with my eyes closed tight, in a pretence of sleep, listening. And then,

'Wilfred, wake up. You've wet the bed.'

I couldn't get up. What could I say? Only, 'I'm sorry, Mummy.' I was ashamed and now I'd been discovered. I would think, *Doesn't Mummy have enough to do, without this? Oh, why can't I get up in time?* I can still hear myself saying sorry through my tears and her saying, 'Don't worry, son. Come and help me with getting these sheets off the bed.' And we'd set to work together in straightening things out.

The curtains now open, the top covers pulled back, I'd pull myself away from the bed of my shame and realise that my pyjamas were soaked.

It's true, then, I'd think, as I hung my head in humiliation. I'd reluctantly grab a sheet, feeling shy, not wanting to meet Mum's eyes. But her manner didn't seem to change and there was some reassurance as she'd bundle up the stained sheets for a wash.

'We'll need to give this bed a good airing,' she'd say, leaving the room.

Chapter 13
Chores

At home Mum's routine consisted of cooking, shopping, washing and ironing.

I remember the knotted bedsheets that Mum would rinse in the kitchen sink at 40 Torbay Road. Her small hands would wring the water out of them by twisting them over and over again until she gave a satisfied sigh, knowing that her job was done. I marvelled at her physical strength.

When I'd get home from school I'd change out of my school clothes and deposit whatever was dirty in a basket located in the corner of our room. On washing day Mum's mood was dependent on the weather. If it were raining she wouldn't have anywhere to dry the clothes which would add to her frustration with life. If it was a fine day – that is, no rain with a slight breeze – then her happiness was a joy to behold. She'd separate our clothes into whites and dark clothing, washing them separately with a soap that when I put it to my nose gave off a strong smell. I didn't have to do any washing while we were living at Auntie's but that would change once we moved.

Mum seemed to do her washing when Auntie wasn't present, so there would be a sort of peace that would reign for the duration. What I loved was that it was just Mum and me. I would stand to the left of her while she soaped up the clothes in the sink and white suds would billow up. Under Mum`s watchful eye, I sometimes scooped up a handful of suds carefully so as not to get them on the floor, which would have invited a concerned look from Mum, as if to say, 'I have enough problems with Auntie, so be careful'. She seemed to be on permanent sentry duty, watchful for any minor infraction that could lead to another argument with Auntie.

Mum would then use a mangle, which was a wooden instrument with rollers in which the clothes were individually placed one by one and water wrung out of them until they were damp to the touch. Mum would allow me to touch one to check before she put all the washed clothes into her basket, along with wooden clothes pegs, and we'd step out into the garden.

The yard was not large, just a narrow strip of earth bordered by wooden fences on three sides. When I thought Mum wasn't looking at me I would spy a gap in the left fence, always intrigued at what I might see, which was not a lot. But as I never saw the neighbours and thought they might have been dead it satisfied me to have the opportunity.

It was a long clothes line but Mum could not use it all. As with everything, she had to share it with Auntie. The stop line – the point beyond which she could not peg any clothes – was invisible to me but well known to Mum. While ensuring I handed the pegs to Mum, who didn't look as she took the next item of clothing, I wondered if her mind was elsewhere, possibly on her relatives.

I knew Mum had family – and Dad for that matter – but the jumble of names and titles for grandparents meant nothing to me. Though when uncles and aunts were mentioned that caught my attention because I could relate to Auntie Carmen and Uncle Norman.

I would take Mum's momentary lack of interest to eye the rest of the garden and spotted in the daylight my other shame, the outside toilet, which had led to many nights of fear and loathing by me for the adults who slept soundly in their beds.

My job was to hand the pegs to Mum as she bent to pick up the clothes and peg them one by one, leaving a gap between each item of clothing.

As I grew older, I too had the responsibility of chores. By a certain age and under Mum's supervision, I would have to carry the white enamel pot, also known as a 'po', to dispose of the overnight pee collected in the pot under the bed on Dad's side. It was a task I hated. Not wanting to look down or smell the stale pee, I would look away and try to work out how long it would take to walk with the 'po' from our room to the outside toilet. Early mornings it was often very cold and sometimes it was raining. I had to carefully lift the 'po' and carry it without spilling the contents anywhere.

I would check to see if anyone was around to avoid embarrassment, and if the coast was clear I would walk swiftly with the contents to the outside toilet. The toilet door had a rusty handle which I thought would fall off if I yanked it too hard. Then I really would have been in trouble with Mum and Auntie. Opening the cracked door, I'd see the toilet was filthy, with cobwebs hanging from the cistern, and a floor that was so very grubby. Then a chain that made a terrible noise even when I pulled it gently. I dared not look too hard at the bowl encrusted with dirt and the toilet seat that looked as if it would disintegrate if you sat on it. I hated this confined space and would rush the 'po' back to our room. Once I'd washed my hands, I could use the bathroom upstairs. There I would try to avert my eyes from the morning detritus left by my cousins. I couldn't stand the sight of any dirt, having seen enough in the downstairs toilet. I would quickly put my hands under the by now cold water, take the bar of soap and rub my hands and the soap together until my hands were no longer visible under the lather I'd created, then rinse them and look for the bit of the towel that was dry to wipe my hands.

Sunday mornings were dull. I had the chore of collecting money from all the adults to buy the *Sunday Mirror*, *News of the World*, *People* and *The Sunday Times*. I felt self-conscious with the jangling coins in my pocket as I stepped into the quiet street and sunshine, looking left and right – but not a car or bus in sight. No noise.

One morning I turned the corner and I saw it, a black dog – and I froze. I was breathing heavily but trying to control the fear in my stomach which was bubbling up to make me run home, feeling foolish. Or would I proceed? I unglued my feet and started across the road, keeping eyes wide open, praying that the dog was not attracted by the coins or felt my fear. I stopped in the middle of the street. *It's not far, you can do it,* I told myself. *The dog's not there*. Moving again, I sped up crossing the road and dashed into the newsagency with relief, handing over the coins. The newsagent smiled as he handed me the papers. *If it's still there, how will I be able to run?* I asked myself. But I had to complete my mission.

I hurried from the shop then cautiously peered around the corner. There was the dog, standing watching me. I pretended not to see it and walked with my head up, making myself feel strong even though I wanted to scream. I walked as calmly as I could and got in through black gate.

Mum in her apron, called, 'Is that you, Wilfred?'

'Yes, Mummy,' I said quietly as I handed her the change.

Chapter 14
Silent understandings

The next afternoon, Mum and I were sitting at the timber din-ing table where both families, Clarke and Roach, would eat to-gether in an uneasy fraternity. The table always had a smooth, white, plain tablecloth stretched its entire length and breadth. Mum was mending one of Dad's shirts with needle and thread with a certain stillness about her, which meant an announce-ment without fanfare was due.

'Wilfred, dry your eyes, we're going out. I've put some clean clothes for you to change into, so hurry.'

'Dry your eyes' was a saying I hated to hear. I would try as hard as I could to stifle my tears whenever they came but it proved too hard so, feeling guilty, I would allow the warm tears to flood my face, ashamed as I turned my head away from Mum's gaze. This crying seemed to last forever. Mum would continue to ask, using words that would give an adult meaning to a child's sadness. Often during these incidents, we were not physically close; there was not a touch of forgiveness from Mum. Just a command to dry my eyes and then we'd speak no more about it – until the next time.

The house that afternoon was quiet, not unusually as my cousins were out and the other adults – Dad, Auntie and Uncle

– were working. Alone with Mum and remembering the incident with the dog, I was upset enough to do what she did not like, let her see me cry. Normally, I wouldn't want to be seen crying outside of our room because I knew this would invite comment from Auntie and affect Mum. But this time Mum and I were alone.

At an indeterminate point in my young life, I came to hate the two phrases that were to dominate the shape and texture of my life: 'Spare the rod and spoil the child' and 'Children should be seen and not heard.' They were the most frequent sayings that I feared, for they were said with menace by adults, even though the words had little meaning to me. But they sounded as if they were meant to deal with some future harm from me.

At home I felt an inevitable emphasis on not being heard. Did I silence myself deliberately? There didn't seem to be any alternative offered by Auntie and Mum, as they would use the 'seen and not heard' phrase often.

I wondered if I were an especially noisy or naughty child. Well, I never really knew! I only knew that I hardly said a word. Muteness was my chosen option. That way I could continue to observe adults at close quarters but remain essentially invisible. This pleased the adults although they made no reference to it. I lost myself in a world of tears and silence.

It was also impressed on me that table manners were always very important. 'Manners maketh the man,' Mummy would say, seizing on a quote for life from the 16th century. It certainly applied when we ate together. In my mind it was also linked to Mum not being at all polite when she and I went to the market and she found bruised fruit and rotting vegetables. She'd give the stallholders 'a piece of her mind'. And she would look for fresh meat, meat that satisfied our palates as Trinidadians and which we often found in Indian shops.

'Wilfred, dinner's ready!'

But I already knew from the smells wafting up from the kitchen that it was ready. I took the knives and forks and placed them in line, as Mum had shown me how to set the table: first the tablecloth, then coasters, knives and forks. Certain items – plates or bowls – were required for different types of food.

'No talking. Adults only. No foul language. Wait to be served. Say thank you!' Good manners were drummed into me.

Certain key foods were placed on the plate. But you could help yourself from bowls of food on the table. There was a large metal pot with a cover, water with various herbs added. Different soups on different days of the week. Provisions bought for Trini recipes – pumpkin, tough skin-peeled to reveal the orange mass, and green bananas that Mum would peel to include in a soup.

'You have to eat!' Dad would say. 'You know how many children are starving in Biafra.' I saw skeletal children on television on the iconic *News-At-Ten* during the civil war in Nigeria, in the late-'60s so I knew what he was talking about. Family conversations were peppered with news and politics.

A cow's heel or pig's trotter would have been chopped up by the butcher and enough brought home by Mum for extra big jars to be found for it to soak and pickle with water, lemon juice and onion. The result was thick fleshy meat with juice which would set me laughing because, with my small hands, I didn't know how to handle it. Dad would hand me a piece on a plate and say, 'You eat it like this,' and I'd try to imitate him, with juice dribbling down my chin as I laughed.

'Look what you've done, boy,' he'd say, as I noticed a big stain on the dining room table. I'd stop laughing. Fingers everywhere, juice running down my chin, watching how the adults were eating.

'Shirley, this is a good piece of pork!' was Dad's regular compliment when we'd eat sous on a Saturday morning with members of both families gathered in the kitchen. After that you wouldn't want any regular breakfast.

After one of these sous breakfasts, a particular scene sticks in my mind. I loved high heel shoes, having taken pleasure early on in the vision of those well-shod visitors to Auntie's kitchen. One day when I was by myself playing with my building blocks, I decided to make a pair of shoes for myself. I found on Daddy's desk a roll of sticky tape and discovered it took no more than three blocks under the heel of my left foot, held together by sticky tape over my ankle, to secure a reasonable facsimile of a high heel. So I did the same again with blocks under my right foot. I stood, then tottered around to see if it would take my weight.

Proud of my design, 'Look, Mummy!' I called out. The faces of the adults in my family changed suddenly, speaking volumes. I winced in amazement. I'd put a lot of effort into creating the shoes and had even tested them out before showing them off. But I could tell from Mum's face that she was embarrassed about something. And Auntie. What was the problem? I didn't want to do it again.

Perhaps my interest in high heels had sprung from imitation of my mother as I spent so much time with her in our small room. Was I a Mummy's boy? I remember how she would call me in on the odd occasion when I'd been allowed outside to play.

'Wilfred, could you come a minute, please?'

From the sound of Mummy's voice, an unpleasant task awaited. It was a chore that mystified me, helping Mum to put on her bra and corset. She would have the brassiere around her breasts as I'd enter the room, averting my gaze. I would have to pull the thinner ends together to get the hooks into the eyes of the clasps with my small fingers pulling hard. The mission successfully complete, there would then be the unpleasant task of helping with the corset. I'd need to apply even greater strength and to me the corset seemed like an instrument of torture. I had to administer the pain – and I didn't like it but couldn't express that.

Chapter 15
Doctors, nurses and kisses

I wanted to play outside like other children but I couldn't, so Mum used to take me to the local park with Mary, who lived across the road. I was not allowed to play with or bring home friends who I met at school, but I could go to Mary's. Her brick house had at first seemed to me dark and best kept away from – until I discovered this was where Mary lived.

When I was about six years old, I didn't have a chance to play with other children outside of school hours unless Mum knew the child's mother. My friend Mary had no brothers or sisters, and we went to the same school. She was taller than me and I noticed she did not have the same skin colour as me. Hers was the colour of Auntie's skin, coffee brown with a lot of milk added.

I sensed sometimes that there were times when Mum would be going off to work but this was not explicitly stated. She would tell me she was going out and Mary's mum would look after me. This felt wrong as I didn't really like Mary's mum. Mum would get me ready, pack a lunch box of my favourite food and then take my hand and walk me the short distance to Mary's house, depositing me with her expressionless mother.

'Now, you be a good boy and I'll be back soon,' Mum would say, which would leave me feeling even more abandoned, knowing that it wasn't true. I'd sometimes be left for hours.

Mary had a play box filled with medical toys: a stethoscope, a doctor's white coat and a nurse's outfit with a hat, and other equipment. *Who am I going to be*, I'd wonder. We'd put a plastic tent up with a Red Cross symbol. *Who's going to be the doctor?* That was already clear to me; as the boy, I'd be the doctor – but I felt uncomfortable about that because of the physical closeness, which I knew my mother would not approve of. Then we proceeded to examine each other – but not for long. At that point we heard the doorbell. Saved by the bell!

But new adventures awaited me.

My presence in the alien school environment did not prevent me from being exposed to what I felt confronted by. Girls were always present. In fact, my early friends were girls, Julie and Mary, as well as boys, Vincent and Ricardo. I remained a shy silent boy, but Julie, who lived locally and whose mother was a friend of my mother, seemed to have taken a shine to me. One day she told me, 'I really like you!' during a playground break. This was of no interest to me.

Julie always seemed keen to touch my skin which wasn't white like hers, but dark. I tried to show her that touching left me uncomfortable, for instance, by moving away from her. But she'd just follow me anyway.

She began to suggest we play her version of 'kiss chase', where one child hides and the other has to shut their eyes and then find the hidden child. If they fail to find them then the loser gets to kiss the winner.

One school day afternoon Julie said we should play the

'kiss chase' game. I demurred, saying that we'd get into trouble, but she insisted. I followed her slowly while looking around for teachers or other children, hoping that we'd be stopped or questioned. Julie found an empty class room full of grey metal chairs, tables and wooden cupboards. Now I understood there was no escape but hoped that a teacher would walk into the classroom and scupper Julie's plan.

No teacher or other child appeared.

'I'm going to hide and you need to count to ten, but shut your eyes,' Julie told me. I shut my eyes after climbing under a nearby table which was large enough to house my sizeable frame. I was nervous but hoping to get this over with, so I stayed where I was.

Julie looked at me intensely. There was nowhere for me to hide. It was now or never – as if there was any doubt. Julie spoke confidently.

I counted softly to myself: one, two, three … up to ten, and then opened my eyes. I looked from under the table and saw a closed door leading out of the classroom to another classroom. I wasn't sure what to do but wanted this game to be over right then. The quickest way was to let Julie have her one kiss and be done. I stayed put and she joined me under the table.

'You have to kiss me now, that's the rule.'

I thought to argue but aged just six, this didn't seem possible against the determined passion of a six-year-old girl. I prepared myself to kiss her.

I closed my eyes, pursed my lips as I had seen actors do in films, and moved my mouth closer to hers. Then in a second it was done.

I had kissed her but in that moment a thought came to me. *I don't like kissing girls. I like boys.* That was it. I told no one.

It took me another fourteen years to act on that thought. But from that moment, I knew I was attracted to boys.

Chapter 16
Hedged in

Snip, snip, snip, I heard, as if my hair was being cut, but without the drama.

It was a Saturday morning in summer and this was the tell-tale noise of Uncle cutting the hedge. The front door was ajar which was unusual as normally it was firmly shut because Auntie would panic if it was left open.

'You can go out onto the path,' Mum told me.

This was a joy because it meant I got a whiff of the strong smell of the green leaves that would fall like rain on the ground as Uncle snipped away in a slow methodical way with what seemed to be huge scissors. I would watch as he'd work his way around the abundant hedge, reducing it steadily to a neat manageable size.

I knew to go beyond the gate was not permitted but I tried to get as close as possible, looking back to see if Mum was lurking and watching. She wasn't. I also realised that there were many people on the street, some of whom would give Uncle a cheery hello as they passed. Sometimes the men would say, 'I see she's got you doing chores,' to which Uncle would only laugh.

I looked up and could see the sky, which wasn't possible

from our room. The house to my right had a hedge growing above a brick wall, making it too high to see over. I'd never heard or seen anyone come from that house, though when Auntie was going at Mum she'd say those neighbours didn't like the overcrowding. 'When are you going to move?' she'd ask Mum pointedly. This only happened when Dad was not around and after these incidents I could see Mum was upset.

During most of my childhood I lived a confined life, snipped back like that hedge, in many ways.

'Wilfred go to your room,' Mum would say, to remind me of the rules: no playing out by the front door or on the street with friends.

One day as I headed home after school, I was hoping that my friend Vincent, who was Irish-born, would notice me and come over to talk. Then, there he was, grinning at me, his face unclean and crooked, with some yellowing teeth showing behind his lips. He presented a sight that I could not associate with friendship, yet I liked him – his rascally nature and the way he would take a dare. The way he spoke and what he spoke about attracted me; not that I wanted to follow him into trouble, but how he spoke pleased me. He was funny and the way he went about things was different than the way others did. I liked to see him, except when he repeated his insistence that we should 'play out', which struck terror in me because I didn't know how to tell him that no, I wasn't allowed to play out. I had a feeling that even if I did ask Mum, 'Can Vincent come in for a glass of water?' she would say no. But what could I do? Get into serious trouble with Mum or lose a friend? My strategy was to say nothing and pray he didn't push to come home with me. That was best, I decided.

Until that one afternoon when, as if he sensed my reluctance, Vincent just kept on walking beside me. He had repeated all afternoon at school, 'I'm coming home with you and I want to play out'.

Those words horrified me as I heard in my head Mum's new mantra, 'You won't play out and don't invite any of your school friends home to us. We don't want the English – they don't like us and they would never invite you home.' Which seemed to be true because, apart from Mary, no friends invited me to their homes.

But Vincent was different. He wanted to be with me and I liked that. I couldn't understand my parents' attitude or find words to argue against them. Vincent persisted, and on our way home I tried to forcibly push him away from me – but this seemed to encourage him. We reached the black gate to my home and I knew the rules applying beyond that point.

So I hurriedly pushed it open, hissing at him, 'Go away, Vincent, please,' as he repeated, 'But why can't I?' He was on the edge of running into the other world, my world, where no one was allowed to see what we said to each other, what we ate, or how we lived – especially if they didn't look like us.

After getting through the gate, I turned around and my spirits rose. Vincent had vanished. I now happily rang the bell and saw Mum's figure moving towards the door. I swept in past her, hoping that I had not imagined the last few minutes. Mum disappeared in the direction of the kitchen, where I could hear Auntie's voice. I rapidly changed into my home clothes and ran upstairs to wash my hands and face. As I came down the stairs, I saw a short figure through the glass of the front door. It was Vincent. I moved rapidly down the hall and, looking over my shoulder, was reassured that both Mum and Auntie had their attention elsewhere, so I opened the door.

'Are you coming out to play?' Vincent hissed.

'No, Vincent. Now please go away!' As I pushed him from the door, still looking over my shoulder, his response was to give me a broad grin and push me back. I grew angry with fright and shut the door. He stood the other side of the door mouthing words I couldn't hear while I prayed he would just go away. I thought Mum wouldn't believe me and say I had brought this little Irish boy to our doorstep, and that all that Auntie had said about the jam jar might be true. Or anything else Auntie might say in the future would be believed.

Then I heard Mum's voice call out, 'Wilfred, who's at the door?'

'No one, Mummy.' I felt a waver in my voice which betrayed my nervousness. But Mum didn't come and I saw that Vincent's shadow had disappeared. I remained for a moment longer to be sure, before moving away from the door.

Chapter 17
Spats and outings

Auntie and Mum would occasionally sit and talk and there seemed no tension between them but soon enough Auntie would say things that would infuriate Mum. My mother was kind and peaceful but when hurt, her mouth would turn down and her brown hazel eyes became dark and menacing. She would not reply, instead waiting until Dad got home after 7 pm each evening to tell him about what Auntie had said.

I was sad for Mum as our lives at 40 Torbay Road seemed to come with so many restrictions. But there were outings, mostly shopping trips, as a relief from the gloom of home.

After chores one Saturday morning when I was seven, Mum asked in a solicitous voice, 'Would you like to go to the cinema?' I didn't understand that you could see the television outside of our home. But once it was explained, the thought of going out to a place I'd never been to was exciting. On that cold Saturday morning, Mum and I walked along the familiar first part of the route, past St John's and on to Kilburn High Road. Then at Milligan's pub, we turned right at the corner and there it was, The Odeon!

When we arrived, at first there wasn't anyone else around. Mum paid for the tickets at the box office and, holding my hand, up a flight of stairs we climbed. Being up in the heights frightened me.

I looked in wonder at the rows of red seats in front of the stage and the heavy red velvet curtains, which reminded me of Auntie's. Then the lights slowly went down and, nervous, I stared at Mummy.

But then I was thrilled to see the curtains opening as if with invisible giant fingers, along with hearing the song, 'When you wish upon a star'. I was lost in the magic of *Snow White and the Seven Dwarfs*. I knew this was a wonderful present given to me by my mother on a Saturday when she had 'a hundred and one things to do'.

When the film finished, to my surprise Mum asked me, 'Would you like an ice cream?'

'Yes, please,' and home we went as I licked. Not knowing that the cinema would be a place I'd frequent decades later.

At other times Mum would announce, 'We're going to the market,' and I would pull on my clothes, making sure that everything about me was spick and span. I'd get our empty trolley and off we'd go to Wembley market on the High Road. As we'd wait for a bus, Mrs this or that would approach Mum and, to my unvoiced annoyance, they would chat without pause. With no encouragement from me, they would then ask me inane questions about school. How I hated the intrusion! What gave them the right to ask me questions? I never spoke about how I felt about this, something telling me that the thoughts I had could not be safely uttered without causing significant offence to all parties.

When we got to the market there would be more ladies with scarves tightly wrapped around their heads and their winter coats bulging. The women were of all heights, sizes and races. Mum would talk on and on. *How does she find so much to talk about*? I'd wonder. Mum had a distinctly sceptical attitude to the daily grind of life and, for her, all men were suspect. Her views frustrated me but I would remain mute.

Not everything was purchased at the market – some goods were delivered to the door.

Our milk bottles stood in a corner waiting expectantly to be put out beside the doorstep. They were made of glass with the dairy logo printed proudly front and back. I knew I had to handle them delicately because there would be trouble if any empty milk bottle was missing from the doorstep when the milkman arrived.

There were two types of bottle: a regular silver top and a red top which was creamy. I knew ours were silver and we would order for the week. It was the only time I could go out independently, only up to the bolted gate, mind you, and I'd wait for Mum or Auntie to come out to pay the milkman who knew everyone by name.

Auntie and Mum had different milk orders, because there were six Clarkes and only four of us.

I would hear the clatter of the milk float, a van with an open section holding both full and empty bottles, as it was driven ever so slowly over partially-asphalted 'cobble stones', which were actually lumps of re-used London bricks. As soon as I heard that sound, I'd run and ask Mum or Auntie for the key to open the door and feel the fresh London morning air. I felt free.

'How are you this morning, sonny?' asked the milkman, in his smart uniform and peaked cap. Shy, I'd look away. I would count the number of milk bottles put down on the step, then Mum would appear with notes and coins for him.

I had a collection of bottle tops. After they'd been washed, Mum would say, 'Do you want these?' and I'd take them, thinking they were as valuable as the paper that adults called money.

One day, Mum and I visited the Town Hall, which was where you went to make a submission for Council housing – and she told me not to tell Auntie. Mum took me along because Dad was working the only times the office was open, so I was company for Mum. I liked the visit because I was with her and were doing something which seemed important, not stuck in that house where I couldn't breathe.

Chapter 18
Moving house

The day started like any other. Dad went to work, Mum helped me get ready for school in the cold atmosphere that often existed between Mum and Auntie continuing unabated, with sniping remarks that often involved me. I strained my ears to catch the odd whispered word between the two, secretly hoping Mum would come out on top. She seemed to maintain steadfast confidence that I would 'always tell the truth'.

'I am expecting a letter about our housing,' she told me that morning, her voice rising in pitch to make clear that she expected that day would satisfy her long-awaited hopes of moving out of our cramped conditions to become the mistress of her own home.

When I arrived home with Mum that afternoon, I could see a letter perched on a shelf near the red telephone. Trying to contain my excitement about what this letter might mean, I touched Mum's arm and she turned and picked it up, carefully examining the envelope. She took me straight to our room and closed the door. Once we were in the room, it was difficult to see because the light had already begun to fade, so Mum reached over and switched on the light, something rarely done. I recalled many times hearing Auntie's accented remonstrations to Dad: 'You know how much electricity costs, so please switch off the light, Clifford.'

I stood quietly, not even changing my school clothes yet, as this was clearly an unusual situation.

Mum stood under the light and opened the envelope, reading slowly while I looked at her face to see whether there were signs of good or bad news. Her face remained a mask as she re-read the contents of the letter. Then finally a rare sighting by me of a smile on her handsome features. It lasted a long time as we two stood alone in the dark room, mother and son. Then as if in a trance, she spoke to the wall.

'It's late. We need to pick up Fidel from Vera,' she said.

I thought Vera wouldn't mind waiting as she had repeatedly told Mum not to worry if she was late, and didn't charge Mum extra. Why not tell me about the letter first, so I could calm that pit in my stomach that was opening up? I touched my belly discreetly as Mum continued to stare at the wall. And I turned my head slightly towards Fidel's cot, hoping she wouldn't see my warm tears. Then without my realising it, she left me standing there, as I heard the heavy door click shut. She had left me alone in that cold dark room, without any word about the news that had made her smile. Abruptly, I stopped crying. I took my jumper and short trousers off and, as I had been taught, neatly folded them, leaving them on the edge of the bed and changing into my home clothes. I sat on Dad's study chair and waited. I couldn't leave the room as Mum had closed the door. The house was silent except for the beating of my heart. Mum returned with Fidel and still didn't say a word to me about what was in the letter. With the instruction, 'Wilfred, look after Fidel while I get dinner,' she was gone.

Dad got home at his usual time, kissing Fidel and me,

which I didn't like. He asked in his normal tone of voice, 'How was school?' The question from a tired man who I'd seen as a shadow ten hours before as he left for work.

Mum poked her head around the corner of the door and spoke quietly. 'Clifford, we got a letter today. Here.' She handed it to him and he nodded, silently indicating that he would read it later.

I helped Dad by putting his shoes under the bed, as he stripped down to a white string vest and shorts. I tried not to look at his body as I was embarrassed at any display of human flesh after his lecture to me years before about seeing your parents naked not being a problem.

Dad finished changing into his home clothes and with his slippers on at last, he finally took the letter from his pocket and scanned it quickly. It appeared to me from his facial response that the content did not surprise him. As Fidel played with his toys, Dad said in a matter of fact tone, 'We're moving. We have an offer of a flat in Wembley'. This was such a clear decision. *If I knew what happiness was, this might be it*, I thought. It was dark outside, and inside except for the single ceiling light flickering dimly.

Dad examined my face. 'Wilfred, Fidel, let's get some dinner before it gets cold.' And with that, we trooped out of the room.

I don't know what the future holds but it has to be better than here, I thought. Although Dad had told me that when we first came to London we'd lived in a place called Ladbroke Grove and Mum had done her shopping for vegetables and fruit at Portobello Market, I only knew of one home before we moved to Chalkhill Estate. And I was very pleased to be headed out of Torbay Road.

On a bright January day in 1970, Mum announced, 'No school today! We're going to see where we'll be living'. I was excited as we took the route to our new home. We caught a train from Kilburn underground station to Wembley Park and I saw the football stadium in the distance. It meant nothing to me as we walked for what seemed forever to get to this new flat. What I saw was a like the face of the moon after watching the Apollo moon landings the previous year. As I looked up at the stadium building that had been completed, it looked odd, with walkways reaching to the sky and concrete mixers here and there. The whole place had a fresh smell but its newness frightened me. I drew closer to Mum. I had come from our familiar box room to a place with so much open space I could see green patches of trees near the railway line, where they were building a new school and a medical centre. I couldn't take it in, while Mum couldn't hide her excitement. So this was the result of those several Town Hall visits we'd made!

The brightness of the day felt as if we were walking on fluffy white clouds. When Mum and I visited the Chalkhill flat we were pleased it was just us that day.

I told my friend Vincent I was leaving the school but told none of the teachers. I reckoned Mum would do that.

Once Mum had told Auntie we'd be moving, Auntie became more, 'Do you need this or that?' Even my cousins seemed rosy, but they always gave that paper stuck in the hole in the window pane a sly look, as if wondering when it would ever be fixed.

Soon it's March 1970, and finally we're moving! Uncle Norman hires a white van and he and Dad, bit by bit, start to empty the room that has been our home. Bed, wardrobe. Mum has already packed up and I've been helping her. Uncle Norman is smiling. Auntie, Mum and Dad say I can go with Uncle to our new home.

Dad calls our new Wembley council apartment building our 'Castle in the Sky' because of the walkways which rise up four storeys, the top called Bluebird Walk. We are in the middle on Greenrigg Walk. For the first time I can see uninterrupted blue sky from our flat. I won't have my own bedroom and will share with Fidel but I don't care. Mum asks me which of the bunk beds I want, upper or lower. I say 'lower.' So that's settled – that's where I will sleep.

We don't have a garden so now I can't play outside the way I did rarely in the Kilburn backyard but this doesn't matter as there's no paper stuffed in the broken window pane. Though the scene that confronts us is daunting, it's like one of the war games I played back in Kilburn, with concrete structures and an open atmosphere everywhere.

It's a strange feeling now to know that we don't have to share a poky bathroom with six other relatives and there's no gas meter to put coins in, because we now have electricity. While Mum keeps an eye on us, we are allowed to play on the rubber-soled doorstep of our new home, there being plenty of room on the walkway to run around – though not play ball games – and look out through the concrete slabs at the opposite block and the carpark which stands to the right of our place.

A few years later when I was a teenager, I had a chance to see our old family room at 40 Torbay Road, Kilburn. The smell which I noticed now, yet had never been very bothered by before, had to do with Auntie and Uncle smoking. I hadn't been to visit for some time and poked around what was now a bedroom for one of my cousins. I looked at the window pane and saw it had been repaired. I looked around the room – it had been redecorated, carpeted and looked very comfortable for one person. As Dad and Mum had said to each other, they could not believe how much stuff of theirs had come out of that small room when they moved, and here I was seven years later, seeing the room renewed, in contrast to the poor state it was in when we'd lived in it. It felt like a bitter dream. We were visiting for the marriage of one of my cousins, Cyprian, and many white people related to the bride, Michelle, were invited. I didn't fancy dancing as I was still too self-conscious though I used to dance with other teenagers, but not in front of adults. I explored the building and found a well-lit room and what I saw astonished me. It was a circle of white people dressed for a wedding but from their murmured whispers, it resembled more a wake. They were so repressed. I was fascinated and drew up a chair – but they seemed not to see me in their midst. *Are they pretending?* I wondered as I gazed at them. Then I noticed that one of the nameless circle would say, 'Would anyone like something to drink?' Someone would reply, 'Yes, I'll have a wine [or cup of tea]', the circle would be broken and then closed, and it would be brought, then the circle would open again for the person bringing the drink, and then close, and that would be it. I sat there as this ritual went on, and I was never asked.

Mum joined me and I whispered to her with incredulity. She uttered one word: 'racism'.

Chapter 19
My new school

I started at the new school in early March 1970. That first day Mum and I walked briskly to the bus stop and she told me in a firm voice, 'You must always take this route home with no dilly-dallying'. Walking that part of the route to the bus stop meant a short-cut along a road with lots of large old houses with gardens and big trees that obscured them. The houses seemed to me to hint at goings-on behind closed doors with not a sign of who lived there, which was very different from Kilburn where the houses were close together. As we walked at a fast pace, I decided that if this was the route Mum wanted me to take, I would keep away from those trees and houses by walking in the middle of the road.

We reached the bus stop and a red '52' bus pulled up. As we stepped onto the platform, 'We'll sit here,' Mum said, pointing to two seats on the lower deck. The conductor in his dark uniform and peaked cap held a silver ticket dispenser, which made a scratching sound as he turned its little black handle. 'Two tickets and we'll get off at the third bus stop,' Mum told him. She gave me the printed paper tickets which I always collected on bus trips – so I was as pleased as could be. Now aged eight, I tried hard to force myself to remember the route, staring intently out of the window. Then I was allowed to give one pull to the wire to notify the driver that we wanted to get off.

As we approach the school gates, we are greeted by a large sign, 'Fryent Infant and Primary School'. It's after 9 am and I neither see nor hear any children. Mum takes my hand as we walk up to what Mum thinks is the reception at the front of a building, but which I think looks like a large barn.

Mum whispers in my ear that it will be alright, but I don't feel it will. I am filled with foreboding. I try to hide my feelings, but tears spill uncontrollably from my eyes. Mum fishes from her coat pocket a handkerchief, handing it to me and waiting for me to dry my eyes and blow my nose, which I do. I glance at Mum. She doesn't smile at me and has a worried look on her face.

Inside, we walk along a short corridor with steps made from very hard grey stone, and then down the stairs to a longer corridor with the same hard stone floor. There are rooms to the left cloaked in darkness and rooms to the right bathed in light. What holds my worried attention is the dark area. As Mum and I sit on cold wooden chairs, we wait for the headmaster. Then from the dark area a man emerges and Mum and I stand up.

'I am Mr Stephens, the headmaster,' he tells us. I manage to remember to say, 'Hello, Mr Stephens,' hoping that I won't need to say anything more. Mum looks at me and says again that it will be alright. No, it won't – but I <u>don't</u> want to disappoint her in any way. She hugs me and then she's gone.

'Come along with me,' Mr Stephens says, leading me to the darkened area. 'Sit here and wait. I won't be long.' He points to a hard wooden bench. As I sit and wait, shuffling my left foot first, then my right, over and over again, there's not a person in sight.

Then Mr Stephens comes back from his office and says, 'Follow me'. Although my feet move, I don't understand what is going on. *Where is my new class?* I wonder. I grow anxious as we approach the bottom of the steps and see a desk and chair which weren't there when Mum and I entered the building, which puzzles me. I can see from what is on the desk that my fears of the wrong committed by teachers at St John's is about to be repeated. The desk is covered with blocks of coloured wood – greens, yellows, reds. I sit down as my heart sinks too. *How am I going to explain this to Mum and Dad? What's wrong with me?* As I survey the mass of blocks, Mr Stephens is speaking but nothing registers with me except fear of failure. I am too embarrassed to ask Mr Stephens what he means and soon, with a smile, he has gone anyway. 'I will be back soon,' he tells me.

I stare at the blocks, pushing one or two to make a shape. I sit in that cold corridor for what seems forever, not knowing what to do. I'm concerned that I'll be seen by my new teachers and the children. *What will they think, seeing me 'the black boy' in the school corridor? They will see me and know I am 'a black* dunce,' I think.

I hear footsteps and soon Mr Stephens is standing beside me. 'How did you go?' he asks, and I have no answer for him.

I felt badly about the exercise but didn't tell my parents. I was taken to my new class and I tried to fit in with the other students but felt a failure once again. It didn't help that my teacher, an Australian called Miss Small, was severe and didn't seem to like me. My only consolation was that I had another teacher, Mrs Pack, who taught me English, and was warm towards all the students, including me. I felt she liked me and encouraged me in English.

One morning about a year after I'd started, we filed into morning assembly and were given the sad news that the headmaster, Mr Stephens, had died of a heart attack. His deputy, Mrs Brandon, a short, fearsome-looking woman who never smiled, had been given the top job.

I remember one afternoon running fast beside a graveyard and realising Mr Stephens was buried there. I imagined him come to greet me with his ghostly pallor, and this served for me to examine my conscience, as I had taken a route away from the usual path to get home. Which meant I was hot and flustered when I eventually got home. Mum enquired with a serious look of annoyance about why it had taken me so long to get home. I lied and not for the first or last time.

The first day I knew my life could change for the worse was a cheerless day in 1971 when my teacher handed me a letter with the instruction, 'Go to the office after school and see the headmistress'. I was terrified, fearing another test.

Mr Stephens had given me a test the year before, and I wondered whether there was a connection between that and him dying. He was the first person I had known who had died so it was a strange feeling. I had dreaded visiting that office ever since.

I stood outside the headmistress's dark door in an alcove and knocked once.

'Come in,' her voice boomed through the door. I entered her office and saw her sitting behind her desk. She had short greying hair, a pale face that seemed menacing to me and no smile. She looked older than Dad. My friends and I knew to keep as far away as possible from her attention. I stood, not looking at her. I was frightened of her and knew she had a letter that I believed would upset my life. She fixed me with a stare.

'Wilfred, I have a letter for your parents. They must get it.'

'Yes, Miss.'

She handed me an envelope that was not sealed, which surprised me for something so important. I took the envelope and left her office.

The school yard was empty; none of my friends were around. I wanted to look at the letter, sensing that it didn't contain good news but needed to get home quickly as Mum would be wondering where I was. It was dark by the time I reached the bus stop. The bus arrived and I bolted to the top deck which was empty, pulled the letter out of my satchel and read it in snatches. It was a request for my parents to attend a meeting with her to discuss my educational needs, specifically that I was having difficulty with reading and maths and that the Education Authority wanted to transfer me to an 'Educationally Subnormal' School (ESN) where my needs could be 'catered for'.[1] I stopped reading and stared out of the window, unable to understand what made me subnormal. This ESN School was a place that one of our neighbour's children, Mandy, attended every school day, being brought home by mini-van.

Ever since the first day I'd attended Fryent in 1970, I had witnessed Mandy being dropped back home, and had thought, 'That won't happen to me'. But now I had a letter to show it would happen unless Dad came to my rescue. *Surely he would see the injustice of this letter*, I thought.

When I got home Mum was in the kitchen peeling vegeta-

---

1 Bernard Coard' 'How the West Indian Child is made Educationally Sub-normal in the British School System' *George Padmore Institute* (1971). https://www.george-padmoreinstitute.org/the-pioneering-years/gallery-of-publications/how-west-indian-child-made-educationally-sub-normal

bles. I handed her the letter. To her question, 'Where have you been?' I answered, 'Mummy I had to see Mrs Brandon and she gave me this letter to hand to you.'

Mum stopped what she was doing and took the letter. 'Bring me my glasses.'

I gave them to her and she read the letter – but her face did not show me if she was upset or not.

'Your father needs to see this when he comes in tonight. You need to get changed now.' And off I went to my room.

Later that evening while I was in my room, the door slightly ajar, I heard my mother say to my father, 'You need to read this.' I waited nervously to hear a reaction from Dad. He called out, 'Wilfred, come here, please.' I saw the letter in his hand as he looked at me and my heart started to race.

'No son of mine is going to an ESN School. I will make an appointment to see her and you will come with me,' he told me. Neither of my parents mentioned the letter over the next few days.

I continued to attend school but felt ashamed to mention the letter to friends or even look sympathetically at Mandy's van pick-ups, making no comment about dunces or idiots, which would have been accompanied by laughter.

A few days later Dad told me an appointment had been made for us to see the headmistress.

The next day I prepared for school as normal but the difference was that for the first time Dad would accompany me to school. I felt protected, but then I also knew Dad could use harsh words and what if he went too far?

When we arrived at the school, the receptionist told Dad to go down the stairs and turn left to Mrs Brandon's office. As we approached her office, I remembered what had occurred with the coloured blocks on that very spot the year before. I looked away.

Dad and I stood outside Mrs Brandon's office door. He seemed to be far away and said little to me. My heart was pounding so loudly I thought the whole school might hear it. I wondered if Dad knew how nervous I was. *How has this ever come about?* I wondered.

'Sit down, Mr Roach, and Wilfred. Thank you for coming this morning to discuss Wilfred's education. As he has made slow progress with his reading and maths, we thought he might benefit from smaller class sizes and more teacher contact than he would get in this school.'

As Mrs Brandon spoke, I kept my head down, but when Dad spoke I looked up and saw that he was gazing out of the window past Mrs Brandon. I stole a quick look at her face. It had changed to a deep red. I looked down again, not wanting to be asked anything.

'Mrs Brandon, I want you to know that Wilfred will not be attending an ESN school – and I will never give my agreement to that.'

The silence that followed had me gripping my legs under my chair waiting to hear who would win, and hoping Dad would. He continued, 'How is it that when Wilfred is home and I give him newspapers to read, 'The Times' and 'Daily Mirror', and I point to sentences for him to read, he manages to do so, yet when he comes to your school, you say he can't read?'

What Mrs Brandon didn't know was that Dad was studying law but wrote on the school parent form that he was a porter with the furniture manufacturer and retailer, Maples. He knew that class really mattered to the English, and he didn't want her to know that she was dealing with an intelligent black man. I did not understand what Dad was telling me but knew he spoke with confidence. Would I ever speak like him, I wondered?

'Perhaps it is your teachers who need to better teach my son, because when he comes to your school, you say he doesn't know how to read or add up.'

I did not hear Mrs Brandon's reply as I focussed on Dad's presence. He seemed to fill the room.

I realised the meeting was coming to an end as Mrs Brandon said, 'So, Mr Roach, Wilfred will not go to an ESN School.'

My relief was tinged with fear that the minute Dad left the school I would start to pay for his victory. Dad stood and I did too, looking at both of them.

'Thank you, Mrs Brandon.'

'Thanks for coming, Mr Roach.'

Her voice didn't seem happy nor did she look at me. Dad and I left the alcove and stood at the spot where I had been given the test. Neither of us spoke as we looked down the corridor that led to my classroom, on the side of the corridor bathed in light. Dad looked at me and I detected no happiness in his voice as he said, 'OK, son, I will see you later. Take care.'

'See you later, Daddy,' I replied dutifully, as he headed out of the school and I went off to join my class.

Chapter 20
Our family Christmas

1970 was the year of the first Christmas in our new home as a complete family unit – Dad, Mum, Fidel, now four and a half, and me eight years old. Dad and Mum would sit at the kitchen table taking bets on the question, 'Will it be a white Christmas or not?' *Aren't adults strange?* I thought. But for my part, I hoped it would be white and Mum would let Fidel and me out so we could build snowmen and throw balls of snow at each other.

That December I knew Christmas wasn't far off because it was so dark, from at least three in the afternoon, and the street-lights would come on not long after. At school, preparations for Christmas advanced with the school Christmas tree covered in bells and paper chains that we had made in art class accompanied by the sound of what was becoming a favourite for me, children singing Christmas carols. I liked to hear my voice among other school friends as we sang, 'Ding dong merrily on high,' and 'Away in a manger,' which always brought tears to my eyes as I sang the words, 'No crib for a bed, the little lord Jesus …'. I used to hope no one noticed.

Soon we were officially on Christmas school holidays but Dad was still working. Christmas Eve morning, all was ready to go. Mum, Fidel and I sat at the kitchen table, Mum shelling peas as we ate our special treat, her delicious home-made coconut bread with butter and ham. The radio blared out Christmas hits like, 'Jingle bells, jingle bells, jingle all the way.' We joined in while we ate our breakfast and Mum busied herself in her own kitchen. I marvelled at how much space she had and felt happy for her. She seemed completely at home now, smiling to comfort us boys. Although I never knew what caused the pain between her and Auntie, I knew somewhere in myself that this was the best outcome ever.

By early evening, we three were sitting in our warm, cosy front room in our assigned places. I used to sit beside Mum on the living room couch and Dad, when he was home, had his own chair. Fidel would jump from Dad to Mum's lap with no restriction. This irked me as I could not recall being allowed such privilege but I kept my thoughts to myself. The television provided yet more 'Christmas cheer'. Mum would tell us with a smile, 'Now you know you have to be good because Santa and his reindeer are on their way with your Christmas presents,' her gentle voice seeming to be even more velvety than usual, like the hot chocolate we sometimes had before bed time. Fidel's face seemed vaguely aware of what she was talking about, whereas I just wanted those presents!

But Dad wasn't with us this evening. I found this odd as I always remembered him being home on Christmas Eve. As I wrestled with this question of his absence – *Where can he be?* – Mum's voice changed from Santa joy to a cold matter-of-fact tone with the words, 'We're going to meet your Dad at Aunt Carmen and Uncle Norman's.' *Go into that cold house? What for?* I thought.

I grabbed Fidel's hand and headed to our bedroom to make

sure I put on my warmest clothing, and Fidel did the same, before we headed out into the winter gloom. We took the train from Wembley Park station where, in the surrounding streets, so many people were doing last-minute Christmas shopping in a bitterly cold wind, while we were headed in the opposite direction. The train having deposited us at Kilburn Station, with its steep descending steps which I hated, we began the long walk to Auntie's. Mum's gloved hand held my hands without mittens, which I also hated, and I held Fidel's little hands tight. Then without warning from Mum, we turned up Dyne Road rather than Kilburn Lane and found ourselves in front of Mum's friend Vera Gascoigne's house. I was so pleased – this really was Christmas! Vera answered the door, her face all smiles, with Sandra standing close behind her. 'Happy Christmas to you all,' they called out, and we all replied, 'Merry Christmas to you!' We laughed together before being welcomed in.

We stayed at Vera's house for what seemed forever, while Mum and Vera caught up on the latest neighbourhood gossip. Vera brought out gifts for all of us and, unnoticed by me, Mum had put some small gifts in her bag which she gave to Vera with a broad smile. They also gave each other Christmas gifts. *Now it's beginning to feel like Christmas*, I thought. Then it was all too quickly over. Vera and Mum said their goodbyes and Vera gave Fidel and me embarrassing kisses.

We left Vera's at a quickened pace, almost running, and arrived at 40 Torbay Road. The heavy draped curtains were closed tight against the winter chill with no light visible from outside through the frosted glass. Something told me that Dad must be there with Auntie and Uncle.

Uncle opened the door, his face wreathed with a warm smile and his deep, baritone voice intoning the words, 'A very merry Christmas to you, Shirley, and boys'. Mum's response seemed not to be as enthusiastic as I'd seen earlier at Vera's. I hoped there would be no tension between her and Auntie.

We spent most of the evening at Auntie's, enjoying a hot drink and cakes in the dining room. My cousins who were now teenagers shared the Christmas spirit, sitting with us for a while before going out for the night. Dad, as was his wont, never ate out and this even included not even eating his sister Carmen's, that is, Auntie's, meals. He made it known that he would never eat out as our Mum's cooking was 'good enough and sufficient' for him, and by implication that should apply to us as well, which it did without opposition from us. Though if Mum took us out, we loved to sample non-Trinidadian food, and even at home sometimes she was not averse to knocking up 'bangers and mash' to my sheer delight.

As we sat in the front room with Auntie's dazzling Christmas tree and presents gathered below, I wondered what sort of Christmas theirs would be without the Roach's presence. As far as I could see, everything was in place, nothing had been moved. Yet the house seemed a mystery to me as if we had never lived there. I needed to go to the toilet and realised that somehow without anyone saying it, things had changed so rather than going straight down the corridor to the outside toilet, I headed up the red carpeted stairs to the bathroom on the landing. It felt so good to be accepted at last, which could not be explained in words.

On the way home it was icy cold and I wondered whether it would snow. Mum and Dad were silent. There was more than just frost in the air as we trudged behind them, Dad and Mum in front not holding hands, and Fidel and I behind them with me firmly holding his.

In the still air, Mum's voice exploded with resentment. 'Why did we have to visit Carmen today? Could we not spend our first Christmas in our own home?'

We went to bed a little later than usual, after a kiss on the cheek. As we lay in our bunk beds, Fidel and I held important conversations about what Santa would bring us, whispered so that Mum and Dad wouldn't hear us, and think we were asleep.

Then we heard a noise and, without saying anything, shut our eyes tight. I kept one eyelid open as I pulled the covers over my head with enough space left to see Dad holding the door open and Mum entering the room. 'Are you asleep?' she asked and I tried not to laugh with excitement, just managing to remain quiet, as did Fidel. She placed a large red Christmas stocking on my bunk head and did the same with Fidel's then slowly closed the door. Well, neither of us moved, and knew that we couldn't open the gifts until later anyway. I had my watch under my pillow and saw it was midnight. Back to sleep.

Awake again, I rubbed my eyes, climbed out of my bunk bed and saw Fidel staring back at me with a smile. I knew he wanted to open his stocking too.

I moved to pull back part of the curtain to see if there was any snow. There it was, a thick white blanket. I opened the window a little and the air was still. Nobody was in sight, just the twinkling of Christmas tree lights in some flats that I could see as looked down on the path freshly trodden on by unknown feet. It was ghostly; I shut the window and returned to the stockings.

Once Fidel had ripped open his stocking, careful not to eat any chocolate, we had to decide what next … We needed to thank Mum and Dad but as I looked at my watch I found it was 3am! We decided to contain our excitement at what Santa had brought us for a little longer.

At some point we entered Dad and Mum's bedroom in darkness, hoping they wouldn't be angry with us. I switched on the light, and with Fidel close behind, we called out, 'Happy Christmas,' jumping on the bed between them. I gave them each a kiss, something I couldn't remember ever having done before, and cried out, 'It's snowing outside!' Mum turned to Dad. 'You win, Clifford,' she said, to which he gave a hearty laugh.

Chapter 21
Fisticuffs

It was a weekday school morning and I woke with one pounding thought, my argument the previous day with Phillip, one of my closest friends. There had been no one present at the end of the school day to witness the heated exchange between us. We had shouted at each other, one pushing the other but no physical blows had been struck. I, being the stockier of we two, would have stood a better chance in any physical confrontation but I recoiled from landing a punch on my fair-headed friend. With the clock ticking, I knew I had to leave as I was expected to pick up my younger brother from infants' school and get home before Mum arrived. I had to go. No more words were uttered – we just glared at each other as if hate was all we had left, walking off in opposite directions. Most school days we'd leave together, laughing about some silly incident that had occurred to us or one of our friends. There had never been anything like this as arguments go, and all over a pack of football cards! This is how it had all started the day before.

The school bell rang for our fifteen-minute break.

Great! I can join the others in the playground for a game of flick cards, I thought.

I hurried to pack my books into myg satchel, and with two

friends, Thomas and Ricardo, ran down Fryent Junior School's stone corridor into a light cool spring day to the tune of shouts from Ricardo, a burly boy with dark skin like mine, and a piercing voice.

'Come on or we'll be late for the match!' We were both aged nine, and had been friends before my arrival at Fryent. We reached the brick wall out of breath but far enough away from the noise of most of the other children to be in our own oasis of enjoyment.

I pushed into the huddle of boys who were gesturing and laughing as one boy readied himself for the contest. Before him a row of eight football cards lined up against the wall showed the crest of the Manchester United Football team. The boy held a single card between his fingers with an eye closed, aiming at the row of cards, and then with a flick sound it flew through the air, hit the cards, but failed to dislodge any.

'Aaah' was the initial reaction from the group, and then we turned on him chanting, 'You lost, you lost, you lost,' the chorus dying to a whisper. The boy who'd picked the 'winning card' off the ground and thrust it into my hand was the owner of the cards, my friend, Phillip. We looked into each other's eyes but neither of us spoke as I placed the card between my fingers, bent my body into a crouch and proceeded to flick the card with vigour as if I were punching someone. It hit the Man U cards, demolishing the display.

'Yes, yes,' the boys shouted. 'He won.'

All except Phillip, whose face had reddened, which meant he was angry. Turning away from him, I accepted the back-slapping from the boys – 'You're great!' – as my smile began to thin and disappear.

I recalled the day my friend Sharon – pale-skinned, slightly taller than me, with sandy blond hair – watched the game from a distance and was curious.

'Why aren't girls allowed to play flick cards?' she asked.

I avoided her gaze. 'Well, it's about football cards and which team you support,' and then, my tone coarsening, 'Girls don't play football do they?' She remained silent but was confused. I hoped this would end what I felt was a pointless discussion, thinking, *Sometimes girls don't get it*, and irritated that I should have to explain this ritual.

'You have a pack of your favourite football team cards, you take some of the cards from your pack, line them up against the wall, your opponent takes a single card and flicks it against the standing cards, and if he knocks them down he wins the other boy's pack of football cards!'

Why would girls care about that? I thought, as if it should be self-evident to her.

Now, the sign for all the boys to return to our classroom was a 'tinkling, tinkling' bell sound as a teacher slowly walked around the playground, ringing the bell by hand.

My enthusiasm of the last fifteen minutes and my excitement about winning had vanished as we walked silently back to our class. The boys called our teacher 'The Kangaroo' on account of her height and being Australian. I had no idea where Australia was, but Miss Small, white as chalk with greying dark hair, was a teacher I grew to dislike. One day her finger grabbed my ear, twisting it repeatedly as she asked, 'Don't you understand?' and I tried to get away from her.

As I entered Miss Small's classroom, I took a chair and desk next to a seated Phillip, whispering to him, 'When can I have the pack of cards I won?'

He ignored me. 'Phillip did you hear me?' There was no

response from him.

As Miss Small announced, 'Class, can you have your book ready?' with her finger poised at the chalk board, I realised he wasn't going to give me his cards. Anger consumed me and I ignored his presence for the rest of that class.

Ever since we'd met on my first day at the school, I'd been struck by Phillip's quiet refusal to do anything he didn't want to do, usually with a silent stare or the words, 'No, Wilfred'. This meant in tone and quiet measure that he had made up his mind. He had told me that he had siblings but they weren't at the school. He had also told me, 'Dad doesn't live with us anymore'. His father had left their home after a row with his Mum.

My family was important to me in a way I could not describe, but although Phillip's Dad wasn't present in his life, that never bothered me even though it did cause concern to other children. Phillip told me he used to be teased: 'You're an orphan, you don't have a Dad'. I remembered what Dad would say to me on a Sunday after lunch, quoting from the Bible, 'Let not you judge lest you be judged by others'. I hoped God didn't judge me for my thoughts, as I knew I was a bad boy. In moments of guilt I searched my thoughts and could find no convincing evidence that he would see me as innocent.

But I felt an increased sense of responsibility and increased feelings of protectiveness towards Phillip as he did not have a father with him. At first I would see him in the playground standing alone and would approach with the words, 'Hello, Phillip,' eyeing him, and he would respond with a simple, 'Hello, Wilfred,' with his eyes to the ground. And so our conversation would follow tentatively. Since we both lived on the same housing estate, I would look out for him and travel home with him on the No. 52 bus and we'd chat about this and that.

I was happy just to be in his company.

Still, I was protective of information about my home, reluctant to talk about what we did there. I remembered Mum's words about 'not discussing our business or washing our dirty linen in public' which was one of her favourite sayings.

I obeyed my mum's repeated strictures about not referring to 'our business' nor inquiring into anyone else's. *Why can't I speak about what we do at home?* I thought. Although I wanted to tell Phillip about my family life, the moment never seemed right, and he remained sad, quietly sad, about his own home life. I fantasised, comforting myself with the thought that as an adult I would be able to say and do exactly what I wanted.

Phillip was taller than me and slim, pale-skinned, with a shock of blond hair. He enticed me with a softly spoken reticence. His voice was gentle in comparison with some of my louder friends like Ricardo, and I had to listen carefully to understand what he said.

I was worried that as Phillip had ignored me at school it would mean the end of our friendship. I couldn't tell Mum. I could never bring friends home or play with them after school. So how could she help? I held onto my feelings of anger towards Phillip. But I missed him.

One morning again not seeing Phillip on the bus to school, I thought about approaching one of our mutual friends to speak to him about the cards. Ricardo, who had been born in London to parents from the Caribbean island of Barbados, came to mind. The thing about Ricardo was that he had no 'off' switch when it came to speaking, particularly in class. He'd talk incessantly in a nasal twang about '... *Dr Who*, and did you see what happened with the Daleks, and I think he should have been exterminated ...'

Miss Small did not appreciate what that meant. She only saw me sitting next to Ricardo, and I was the one called up to explain why I was talking. I stammered, 'Well, you see Miss ...'

That was enough. 'Wilfred, go and stand in the dunce's corner and turn your back until I say you can turn round.'

This humiliation usually lasted the remainder of the lesson. I swore never to speak to Ricardo again but always did. He had such an irresistible smile and story to tell.

No, I thought. Ricardo can't help. I'll have to sort this out myself. My other friend, Thomas, told me that disputes over the cards were resolved by both boys fighting it out in the school sandpit at the end of the school day. The sandpit was located at the end of the playground, built high off the ground. There was a significant risk of being caught by the headmistress, Mrs Brandon, or even being caned with a long thin piece of wood applied to the backside or on your hand. Whatever the punishment, it would be followed up with a written letter to your parents.

To use my fists to resolve my dispute with Phillip seemed silly but I felt hurt and thought this act of physical violence might take the emotional pain away. I steeled myself to go up to Phillip during the lunchbreak in the school playground. He was standing by himself in deep thought. I wondered whether he was thinking about the 'incident'.

As I approached he pretended, by turning his head away from me, that he had not seen me. When the moment came, I tried hard to look at his face but found it difficult and kept looking away too. But I managed to tell him I was not happy about the flick card game and wanted to resolve it with a fight after school.

'Would you come?' I asked.

After a short hesitation he said, 'Yes,' in the soft voice I had come to know and like. I thought *This is it*, as I swiftly walked away, feeling a sort of happiness mixed with fear and asking myself, *Can I really do this ...?*

But my thoughts ran on to the words, *'... do this to my friend, Phillip?'* I had my doubts but I was determined to go through with it.

Phillip and I both understood that we'd meet in the sandpit after school but before 5 pm and I had to use my cunning to evade any teacher. It was understood that if you didn't show up then you had 'bottled it', which meant the other person had won the argument and it was settled in favour of the one who had turned up.

As I hid in the boys' toilet, I was sure just by this action I would not 'bottle' it and as I waited I realised that I would be late home. So Mum would know something was wrong. I always followed Mum's rules to the letter, never overtly questioning her unquestionable authority. But here I was hiding in the toilets, evading Mrs Brandon and every other teacher. So I put an iron fence in my mind between that heavy concern and what I was getting myself involved in. If I was caught, I would get at least the cane and also lose a friendship. But I didn't really know what else I could do about the situation.

It's now or never, I thought as I sensed it was time for me to leave the toilets. I stealthily muffled the sound of my breathing and footsteps as I left the toilet. I looked around, and with not a soul in sight, I focussed on the quickest way to get out of the school block and to the sandpit.

I also seemed at that moment to have a remarkable freedom that did not exist for me in the school day – that is, I could go where I wanted and no one would stop me or ask me questions. Before I knew it, I was at the edge of the sand-pit, which was boarded high by wooden beams, and could be seen from Miss Brandon's office even though it was located on the edge of the playing field.

I didn't think she was in the office, but still you never knew. The old girl sometimes appeared seemingly out of thin air with a nasty look on her face.

The minutes hung heavily and then in one bewitched moment, Phillip was standing in front of me. We were alone – no other kids were there to witness our 'showdown'.

I felt myself soften as I gazed at him but then corrected myself, remembering why I was there. Without a word I stepped into the sandpit. Phillip followed. The scene resembled those boxing matches, Muhammed Ali vs. Jo Frazier, favoured by Dad and Mum, which we had to watch as a family, the only upside being that I got to stay up late!

Now that I was steeled to fight, I put my fists up. They had the capacity to seriously hurt someone taller than me, even as tall as Phillip. This worried me but I could not turn back now. I stood and waited. I realised that despite all my anger at the idiocies and injustices that adults had perpetrated against me, I had never hit anyone. I always took it out on myself, I thought, and at this moment my tears began to flow.

I recalled one of Dad's Sunday stories of a great uncle in his twenties who was a 'huge' man and had sworn at his mother, who was a small woman. Dad said she threatened to hit him with her hand, and he said, 'Mama, if you wish to hit me then I shall keep my hands at my side like a gentleman'. And here I was wanting to strike a dear friend!

Then my words came *sotto voce* addressed to Phillip. 'I'm going to lower my arms and if you want to hit me, that's fine,

I will keep my hands by my side'. I added, 'You are my friend and I could never hurt you'.

With a great sense of relief, I rested my arms by my side. Tears came to my eyes again and to Phillip's, who had said nothing up to that moment.

'I am your friend, and sorry,' I continued.

Phillip regarded me for a moment with both his fists held high. He did not reply but slowly lowered his fists and started to cry. We each moved towards the other in the middle of the sandpit and we embraced, holding each other tight – I with my eyes shut. Then after what seemed a long time, we moved apart, looked at each and laughed. In that moment I knew our friendship was as solid as could be, and we walked away, arms wrapped around each, laughing together at the two days of nonsense.

Chapter 22
Bunking off school

I had been at Fryent Road for a year. I didn't like the school or the teachers. I always felt, after that first test in the corridor, that they couldn't be trusted. Mr Stephens had seemed like a fair man but had treated me badly and I couldn't forget it. Then the new headmistress was an angry woman who seemed keen to use detention and the cane, so that I wondered whether she even liked children.

I hated school and one day I just left the grounds. The register was always taken at the beginning of the school day once you'd gone to your house group and then off to your first lesson. *That's when I'll do it*, I thought. *I'll just walk as calmly as I can out of the school gate.* I hid in Chalkhill and felt rather foolish, but couldn't turn back, and stayed away the whole day. I felt guilty.

I knew Mum would pick Fidel up from the primary school and then head home by 3.30 pm, so I had to aim to be there from then. I was starving but couldn't go to the local shop run by a Norwegian guy and his wife who were so racist they used to threaten to call the local Beat Bobby, a huge elephant of a man who'd think nothing of clipping your ears and then dragging you by the ears all the way to your parents' door. I had seen him do it and vowed it wouldn't happen to me.

Where to go? I headed for home, familiar territory, and found a cupboard in the bin sheds outside our block of flats. I peeked out of the cupboard. It smelt bad but I thought *This feels safer than outside*. My heart wouldn't stop pounding like a steam engine for some time. Then I settled in for the afternoon.

As I waited it out there, what I considered to be an 'adult' idea came to me. *This is silly*, I thought. *Maybe I should go home*. But I had to make up a story in case I met Mum on the way. I decided I'd tell her I was sick. It had to be something she believed, and if I said I didn't like school I'd get a telling off. I didn't want to let her down.

As I went up to our flat, I wondered whether this transgression of mine would be discovered despite my best efforts. I knew concealment was an art form, given there were truant officers from the school authorities who could visit your parents' home or send letters by post to confirm your absence.

I got home before Mum and changed into my home clothes, nervous that I'd be discovered. I started to read a book but couldn't keep up with it. Then I heard the key in the door, rushed to the bottom of our darkened stairs and started to walk up them, readying myself with excuses as to why I'd bunked off school, when I heard crying. I looked up to see Mummy crying. I froze. I'd never seen her cry before. Now she had tears running down her face. I knew she had a mother so thought she'd died. Mum came down the stairs and nothing more was said about why she was crying or my bunk off from school. I'd find out many years later why she was crying – her brother had died.

So my parents never found out I'd skipped school. I never

could understand why my parents didn't know about that un-happy event – but then you never knew what they did or didn't know. It was just what they chose to reveal.

The one bright spot at school were my friends, Vincent – who'd transferred from St John's – Ricardo, Phillip, and one or two others. But I felt so responsible for what did or didn't happen about my performance level in class that it was hard for me to feel safe or relaxed. I always felt as if I was going to be sick.

Bunking off school – this was something that white kids did, not black kids. Just knowing what could happen with my parents was enough to put the lid on that idea in future.

So what other tricks did I get up to instead?

School sport – whether learning to swim or not, we got the chance to leave the school environs for sport. In swimming, if we were successful we'd get a certificate.

Stealing pornography? Not for me. There was nothing to see except a bit of bare flesh on the telly. The rest was left to my imagination.

Chapter 23
School hols

Come the school holidays in late July 1972, I was aged about ten. We school friends all said goodbye to each other and then came the embarrassing question: 'What will you do in the holidays?' I hadn't any idea and was rather embarrassed by my ignorance. Mum had mentioned we'd go out; that wasn't in my hands but hers. I knew Wembley existed and where we'd lived before, where Kilburn was, and trips with Mum by the train to see one of her friends, but that was it. Where was this great big world? Did I really want to be part of it? School was big enough, I thought.

Then one day in the holidays I was on my first visit to Central London on the Underground. Smoke hung in the air, the seats were red and the handles shone. I looked about the train as we entered a dark tunnel and I became fearful of this new experience. Did Mum know where she was going? Would we be alright? OK, Mum said we were to get off at the next stop so I gathered my belongings and stood holding the metal bar, waiting for the lumbering train to emerge from the dark tunnel into the light of an Underground station and platforms.

Soon we were standing outside Buck House. We watched passively as the soldiers marched along in their black bear hats, like bears' heads but without the eyes. In their red tunics and with rifles held stiffly, it didn't look like much fun to me. So there were the two of us, standing in a group gawking at the palace, and I thought we looked so different from the others. Mum seemed to be somewhere else, dreaming.

We went into a green park beside the palace and found a shady spot which was damp and had dog poo. Mum had brought Eccles cakes which she'd baked. They were sold in supermarkets in the 1960s and I still like them to this day. It wasn't the currants in these small cakes that I liked, so much as the way the cakes were topped with brown sugar, which accentuated the soft pastry inside and the sweet crunchiness on the outside.

It hadn't taken us long after moving to Fryent Road to find the local market and, of all places, it was under the iconic football stadium at Wembley.

So in the school holidays that was always an outing, of sorts. It was a new market and we'd take the trolley. It wasn't that I was annoyed with Mum about that, it was that everything came down to me, to my help. What about Fidel? Or Dad? But these were discussion no-go areas. I had to help and that was that. I thought it was too much for me, but I would bite my lip and get ready. This time would we take the dreadful implement called the trolley which I would have to drag back home? It was all part of my training, I knew. There was no specific end result I wished for, or any discussed. This was what you did and no questions asked.

One Friday Mum announced that we'd be going to the market at the crack of dawn on the Sunday, and as the oldest son, as usual, there would only be me to help her. This particular Sunday morning I knew I had to get up and dressed early.

I looked at the little clock at the side of my bed. It said 6.30 am, and I wondered whether it would be Portobello Road that day. Or Petticoat Lane, so Mum could get fabrics for new dress designs or wool to crochet or knit while watching Coronation Street. The thing that bothered me was the distance and the load we would have to bring back – veg, fruit and meat, or fabrics. It would take the best part of a day, and for me the trip would become unbearable if it snowed or rained heavily. But to Mum, come rain, hail or sunshine, she would be out there and so would I, bringing back what was needed for the family.

If it were possible to get more warmth and security out of that heavy striped yellow-and-pink sheet and blanket then I would have, but I didn't want Mum switching on the bedroom light and cheerfully intoning, 'Wakey, wakey'. So, as my feet touched the floor, I tasted the inside of my mouth, feeling that I needed to brush my teeth, then sniffed under my arms. *Pooh*, I giggled to myself quietly, then stopped to hear Fidel's gentle breathing, which told me he was still asleep. A quick peak into the top bunk confirmed it. Mum had told me, 'Don't wake Fidel …' but I'd failed to hear the rest for I knew it off by heart, '… until it's time for him to get up'. The night before I had laid out the clothes I was going to wear to the market on my chair, as if I was my own butler, really. I went to dress in the bathroom and as I opened the door I noticed light flooding through from the kitchen, and knew Mum was up and would be pleased that I was too, as this was evidence of her influence.

Then in the kitchen Mum provided me with a little cereal. Sometimes she would be preparing some meal or other and without warning would burst into melodic verse poetry almost as if she were singing a tune she'd stored away and was dusting it down to see if it still held a note. This morning she stood at the kitchen sink and recited in song.

'Where's Daddy? I asked when she'd finished. 'Oh, he's gone out for a walk to buy the newspapers.' The day was getting better by the minute as this was a job I would not have to do.

Once we were ready to leave, Mum stood for a moment regarding me, doing a quick check of how I was dressed. She stood in a formidable pose with a heavy winter coat, shoes and stockings. I had my woolly hat on, a heavy winter jacket and boots. Mum also had the shopping trolley, and as soon as we were out the door, without a word she handed it to me and I took it dutifully. The cold air grabbed my hand in its icy grip and attacked the exposed parts of my freshly greased skin. I would always wonder whether I'd put enough cream on, concerned that my face wouldn't last a lifetime due to its delicacy.

'We'll walk down to the stadium,' Mum told me, and my relief was palpable as I thought about the short distance to haul home our shopping later in the day.

On other days we'd head for Portobello Market or Petticoat Lane. West Indian mothers and their trolleys! I grew to hate Mum's trolley with a passion. It became my job to lug it unfair distances to and from markets, while I focussed on missing pedestrians' toes. Their owners would be quick to give me a racist insult or insolent stare. Sometimes bus conductors would not stop for us, or if they did and saw the trolley, it was a given that there would be an argument over their orders not to 'block the gangway'. I sensed the tone only applied to people like my mother with dark skin, a scarf and hair neatly arranged. And why did this always happen on a day when it was raining or snow had just fallen? Some days I just hated going out with Mum but I never told her. I was always afraid for her safety.

But what could I do, being so small, I reasoned? I suspect she was always more concerned for my safety than she ever was for her own, both on and off the buses.

At the Portobello food market, trays of fresh produce would gleam in the chill winter air. As we walked at a steady pace down the hill to the market, I'd watch for Mum to cross the road safely and she would put on the glacial face that portrayed not a hint of her true feelings. I pretended at that early age not to notice but my early disposition and need for survival gave me an acute understanding of Mum's and other Caribbean adults' dispositions.

Mum haggled with the English stall holders over piles of fruit and vegetables and to my embarrassment dug into those piles with her small but nimble fingers to pull out unbruised apples or potatoes, much to the visible horror of the stall holders. They would reach over a protective hand, as if to say to Mum, 'You can't do that!' and as I watched on helplessly by her side, she'd respond in a firm and telling voice that I knew so well, but they didn't.

'I know you keep the best at the bottom, so don't you be giving me that nonsense,' she'd say. And with that, she'd pick up the piece she wanted and calmly ask, 'How much a pound for this?' holding up the healthy specimen. By this time other women would see what was happening and slowly inch their way towards Mum to see if they could follow her example.

I did not dare look up at the dejected stall holder who would give her a good price, calling her 'Madam'. Next thing I'd hear the noise of a brown paper bag joining the other purchases in the trolley and Mum coolly instructing me to, 'Come, chile,' as I tugged that damn trolley to the next battlefield.

Chapter 24
Baby brother no. 2

By late-1972, I was well and truly settled in our new flat at Greenrigg Walk although I was unfamiliar with the 'walk-ways' themselves. Mum had shown me a familiar route out to the street which I in turn had to teach Fidel. He was four years younger than me and uncooperative and obstinate by nature.

Having worn an eye patch to correct a squint since he was a baby, he never felt truly at home in the world, was my view. He was always saying, 'No!' to me, and Mum would come down on me 'like a ton of bricks' for one tiny infraction by him. I had to know with all my ten years of childhood experience how to get him to do something he didn't want to do, like read a book, and if I didn't then the problem must have been because I wasn't doing it correctly. So I had many quiet cries where no one – neither Fidel, Dad nor Mum – could see me. I understood where Mum was coming from but couldn't she see that I was a child too, and that sometimes your younger brother just doesn't want to oblige and feels perfectly within his rights to ruin your life? So I soldiered on only to learn one day, as I was helping Mum in the kitchen, that her stomach had grown ominously larger and that she was going to have 'another baby'. I didn't understand or care where this baby had come from but knew without doubt that it would mean more work for me.

Another morning after breakfast, just before Christmas, Mum announced that Fidel and I were going with her to visit the hospital, '… where I'll give birth to your baby brother,' she said. It was the first time I had heard her mention the sex of the baby. I felt Fidel was enough to cope with and was not happy at another arrival.

I didn't want Mum to make the trip but of course couldn't tell her that as what I saw before me was a woman with a large stomach, which made me feel sick. Sometimes she would ask me to put my hand on her stomach, or she would say she needed to walk very slowly and would be out of breath. I would ask myself, *What if she suddenly has the baby in the street?* I thought Mum really wasn't thinking about me or Fidel. What was the need to take us to the hospital? And why had she stayed in St Mary's Hospital for an operation the previous year? That terrible experience had convinced me I should have as little to do with hospitals as I could.

We dressed in our familiar winter clothing: us boys in boots, jeans and jumpers and Mum with her big coat and flat-heeled shoes, a scarf around her dark hair, and her bag.

We left the flat to be met on our walkway by a cold flat day, with no one around. Thankfully, that morning there was no ice underfoot. We took the 'coffin lift', called that because it had just one tiny window too high for me to see out of, and then took a short cut to Wembley Park Underground station entrance. As I waited for Mum to buy the rail tickets, I looked back at Wembley Stadium, wondering what was inside as I had never been there. It looked like an old cake with crumbling grey icing.

As we walked down the twenty stairs, I wondered whether Mum would stumble as Fidel reluctantly held my hand. Mum sat down with relief on a platform seat and the station master announced, 'The Metro is due to arrive shortly. All stations to Harrow on the Hill.' I wondered what was at Harrow on the Hill and whether it was a large hill, hoping Mum would take me there one day.

Our rumbling Metropolitan Line train arrived and its old doors were stiff and heavy for me to open. Mum got on first, then Fidel, and I pulled the door hard shut. I was watching Mum, with her large stomach, who did seem more concerned for us than herself. I just wanted to protect her and make things easier for her. About fifteen minutes later, we arrived at Northwick Park and went down a set of steep steps and then walked by the fenced path to reach the hospital.

The hospital grounds had many grey shell-like buildings and paths that led nowhere, and the winter air was thick with the smell of concrete. I was glad when we got to our final destination, the maternity ward. I knew about maternity hospitals from the memory of being taken by Dad to see baby Fidel when he was born. More recently, Mum had also taken me every day during the long school summer break to St Mary's Hospital in Paddington where she worked as a laboratory cleaner. I had met her boss Dr Ward, a kindly man who seemed to like my Mum. Afterwards she'd taken me to a small room with a table piled high with *Women's Weekly* and *Women's World* magazines, telling me to sit in one of two comfy plastic chairs and read the magazines and that she'd be back soon. So I went through the pile of magazines looking for stories about kings and queens and I found one about Emperor Haile Selassie and was very happy, turning each page with silent excitement regarding his wealth and court rituals.

We followed Mum into a building marked 'Maternity Unit'. It felt to me as if we were at last getting somewhere. There was a woman sitting behind a desk. She didn't smile but looked at Mum and asked, 'Can I help you?'

'I'd like to show my sons where my baby will be born.'

The woman with no name looked over the counter as if she had not seen us, then seemed to grow softer and spoke gently. 'Of course, go right ahead.' We walked in and I felt a lot happier about my mother staying there to have our baby.

By early January 1973, Mum was still in hospital and we were back at school. I knew she wouldn't be home to greet Fidel and me or to collect him from school. That would be my responsibility. I had not wanted to do that but Mum said, as she and Dad were leaving for the hospital, 'Now I expect you to take care of your brother and Daddy while I am away. Take care of yourself'. Then she was gone, and I didn't know when I would see her again.

So now we had a home without a mother.

I was responsible for the care of Fidel after school until Dad got home from work or university, which meant I would get to stay up until then, but Fidel had to go to bed at the usual time. I knew I couldn't be late to pick him up from school so my friends would get a quick brush-off at the school gate as I rushed to catch the earlier Number 52 bus and sat nervously counting the stops until I could ring the metal wire and hop off.

I would get there just in time as the school bell rang, a message that the school day was at an end. Whereas I felt my day was just beginning.

Though Fidel's school was reasonably close to our tower block home, I had no confidence that I could handle any crisis connected with him, such as if he ran away or ran onto the road. After school, I saw him standing by himself in the schoolyard in his grey shorts and tightly buttoned-up dark wool coat. *Dressed like that he looks so sad*, I thought, and for a moment it reminded me of what I felt like most of the time. His shoes were scruffy and his laces were not completely done up. *If Mum could see this she would have a fit*, was my next thought. *Well, at least that takes the heat off me for now, because she can't see him from hospital.*

I had the impression that Fidel did not have an overwhelmingly admirable view of me, shown by his unwillingness to behave, always tugging and pulling away from me. He would shout, 'You're not Mum,' and I felt terrible as I knew I wasn't, but what choice did I have? Then I'd get angry and would pull him closer to me, and then a tug of war, with me winning, but at what cost? Making my life hell. It didn't help that Mum was forever talking about 'setting a good example for your brother so that he doesn't grow up to be a thief.' I was at a loss to understand how not walking in dog poo, which he seemed awfully keen to do in my company, would somehow make him a bad person. Well, I knew there was no point telling her that she was wrong. Once I tried to find my voice to say, 'It's not fair,' – that being about as much as I could safely manage – but as the words caught in my throat she told me I was being insolent. Words of dissent such as, 'I can't,' 'I don't like it,' and, 'Why can't we?' would never again pass my lips.

I'd offer my open palm for Fidel to hold hands but he'd refuse. But I'd get him home via the route Mum had told me to follow, with him following me dutifully in the dark of the winter afternoon. We had to decide whether to take the least harrowing route which was either via four flights of dimly lit stairs

– where we were unsure what or who was going up or down – or take the lift which Mum and I had christened 'the coffin'. It had a slight odour which led to a nasty taste in my mouth, like an old rag, and a ceiling light as if it was a prison cell, encased in striped, ribbed silvery metal. It would take forever to come and then to reach its intended destination, creaking in a way that struck terror into my heart. *What if it stops and we can't be rescued? Or if Fidel has an uncontrollable temper tantrum?*

To avoid the stairs and whoever we might meet on them, I decided we'd risk the unreliable 'joke of a lift', the coffin. We got in, I pressed the button to the third floor, and to our surprise, nothing happened. Then, just as I was about to fall in a crying heap on the floor, the lift creaked into action. By the time we reached our walkway landing, the lighting for the long corridor was on.

Home at last, I thought, even though the coldness and silence of the flat disturbed me. There was no Mum or Dad present and I was at a loss about what to do next. *I have never faced this situation aged ten years old*, I told myself.

I battled with Fidel about his clothes strewn across the corridor floor leading to our bedroom. I so wanted to hit that boy, this being my moment of maximum dislike for him, but I turned and waited for a moment. Then I asked, in the calmest voice I could summon, for him to put his clothes away. He did. Then without a glance at me, he came out, walked to the front room, opened the door wide so I could see him, and plonked his bottom on Dad's favourite chair. He then got the television remote control, switched it on and proceeded to watch our favourite afternoon show, *Lost in Space*. I was relieved that in some ways Fidel was quite self-sufficient and on this occasion it would work well because he couldn't really help me in my next task, preparing our evening meal.

I realised there was no time to spare as Dad would be home soon and I knew from being with Mum at this time, around 5.30 pm, that she would have been preparing the rice for us, and spaghetti for Dad, which he preferred. These dishes would be accompanied by a meat and vegetables dish.

I hurriedly changed out of my school clothes into my home clothes and entered our kitchen, or as I thought of it, Mum's kitchen.

I stood looking at the beige cupboards, trying to remember where the pots were that Mum used. I proceeded to find a large silver pot with a small handle, then turned on the electric cooker, added water and some salt to the pot and placed it on the electric ring, waiting for it to boil.

There was a kitchen clock and, looking at it anxiously, I wanted everything to be ready by the time Dad turned up, just as Mum would have arranged. I wasn't great at telling the time but thought it might take twenty minutes for the rice to cook.

Nor was I sure how to cook the meat that Mum had left in the fridge but thought, *Dad will be fine with whatever I cook so long as it isn't overcooked.* So I washed the rice the way I'd seen my mother do it, then scooped the rice into the boiling pot, avoiding any hot water splashes.

As the pot boiled away, I was suddenly worried about why Fidel was so quiet, wildly imagining he'd fallen out of the window, or had got Mum's favourite lipstick or perfume and smothered himself in it.

I left the boiling rice and located him in the front room still watching television. Mum would have banished us to our bedroom but she wasn't home, so I felt a peaceful approach would be to leave Fidel alone. I went back to the kitchen and the rice was ready so I found a colander and tipped it so that it came out as a hot steaming mess.

Then I heard a key in the front door lock. It was Daddy. We both left what we were doing and waited expectantly for Dad to walk down the stairs with news of Mummy. The second Dad's feet hit the hallway, Fidel's hands were around Dad's legs so he could not move. He laughed, picked up Fidel and hugged him, asking, 'Have you been a good boy?' and looked at me for confirmation.

'Yes, he helped me with dinner,' I lied, to which Dad exclaimed, 'Dinner?' I thought he was going to cry, but nothing came.

He hurriedly took off his hat and overcoat but I noticed he did not follow his usual routine of changing into his home clothes of pyjamas and slippers. He remained in his work clothes.

I returned to the rice and then remembered that Dad did not eat rice. It was too late. Dad was already sitting at the kitchen table waiting for his meal. I suddenly felt ashamed that I had forgotten and had cooked this mess of a meal for him.

As we sat at the table, Dad still didn't mention Mum, nor did he comment on eating the rice, as he took mouthfuls using his spoon. We ate in silence. Then as the last spoonsful of rice were finished off, Dad looked directly at me. 'I am very proud of you, son, that you cooked this meal, and even though I don't like rice I was happy to eat it,' he said. My heart swelled. Dad had praised me. I couldn't reply, and feeling that I was going to cry, put my head down, wondering what Mummy would say.

Dad got up from the dining table, put his plate in the sink and disappeared. I cleaned up the kitchen with Fidel's help and just as we had finished, Dad appeared in the doorway, which I knew as the signal that he was going out. I wondered in those few seconds where he was going. He was wearing his flat cap and heavy winter coat with the big buttons, which were unbuttoned at the top.

Then he spoke as if unsure whether to tell us anything or not. 'I am going to the hospital to see your mother, as she hasn't had the baby yet and she's in a coma. I don't know if she will make it.'

As his words sunk in, Dad said, 'Goodbye sons,' and closed the front door. I pulled Fidel close to me and we went into the front room until it was Fidel's bedtime.

Dad had seemed so fallen when he spoke. I wanted to make it better but I didn't know how. After I put Fidel to bed, I switched off the hall light, went to the front room and sat by myself, feeling abandoned by an adult world full of mystery. No one ever explained anything. I looked around instinctively to check whether anyone was there and then I started to cry. I went to bed not knowing if I should wake up the next morning to my world destroyed, or with a mother and a new baby brother.

Chapter 25
Home responsibilities with siblings

The next evening Dad took us to see Mum and baby Herman in the hospital.

A few days later Uncle Norman brought Mum home from hospital, along with Dad and our new baby.

Seeing Uncle was always a plus. Oh, how I looked forward to my buccaneer uncle turning up at our home, wafting cigar smells and the like, with loud gutful laughter and a twinkle in his eye. I adored him as much as I understood the concept of 'Uncle' – a man who gave advice and support, warning you not telling you, and starting to treat you as an adult, bringing gifts and even footing the bill. Kind of like a dad without complications.

I felt the excitement of the day but also unease. What would this new creature, the baby, mean in our lives? After all, Mum, Dad, Fidel were well-known to me, there was a structure, a rhythm to our lives, but this new baby changed all that with constant needs to be kept warm, fed, and have nappies changed. I looked deep into the future and all I could see was more responsibility for me. It felt like a dud deal to me. Then there was the name 'Herman'. *Herman* – the name echoed in my head. I separated the syllables. 'Her' 'man'. *Have my par-*

ents gone mad? How can I tell my friends that my new baby brother is called Herman? It's so German. Do we have secret German relations that I know nothing about?* I decided the wiser course of action was to stay silent and keep my thoughts to myself.

Mum roped me into service. As my eleventh birthday rolled around, I could no longer escape. How to sterilise the bottles? That smell became oh so familiar to me. Making sure baby was warm. But how would I know? Just to pick up this delicate thing with a big head and hairy fat arms and chubby legs was a marvel. Fidel and I used to touch him or just watch him sleeping. Mum's bedroom became the nerve centre for all that was 'baby'; in fact, the whole household revolved around baby, his smells, his eyes, his moving, his sleeping.

Meanwhile there were duties for me: off to the shops, taking the shopping list; Saturday cleaning; helping Mum prepare meals; and before long I would start to be given the responsibility of preparing full meals.

One day a midwife arrived after Mum was in great pain from her caesarean section operation.

I took her to my mother's room and as I withdrew I caught a glimpse of Mum that I had not seen before. I saw her vulnerable and in need of care.

The room was always heated now, smelt of Dettol and there was cotton wool on the floor and bedcovers. It was like Mum's hospital bed, only this was at home.

Mum beckoned me over and pulled back the sheet. I saw a huge scar. Mum had had her belly cut open, running down from above her belly button. I saw this and I was determined not to look away from what had been a brutal massacre of my mother's stomach, a savage cut as if someone had ripped it open. After a moment, I winced and turned away. Mum said, 'This is what caesarean section is'.

I felt for my mother. And in a more selfish way, I felt for myself – and my increasing family responsibilities. And prime among them was keeping a check on Fidel.

One day the following year, I spotted Fidel carrying a suit-case and wearing his best suit. He was heading over Wembley Park Bridge, down the hill, and he had a determined stride that I knew so well. Finally, I caught up with him and, almost out of breath, I asked him, 'And where do you think you're going?'

Mum and baby Herman had gone for a walk to the shops while I was left to care for Fidel. I'd told him to stay in the front room while I was doing homework in our bedroom, keep-ing the door ajar. But I lost track of time. I realised that the house was very quiet, too quiet, and called out to Fidel. There was no response. I'd started to panic but thought he might be hiding somewhere in the flat. I'd searched every corner of the flat but there was no sign of him. He was gone. Thank God I found him. I was the one who would have had to face the con-sequences from Mum.

By the age of twelve I had a growing interest in what was happening in the world even though I could not go anywhere on my own which I yearned for. My little transistor radio pro-vided an ear to a wider world but 1974 ended quietly in our closed family circle with a traditional Christmas. The stuff of life was becoming clearer to me by the day – and my interest in current affairs was growing: mostly about politics and Prime Minister Edward Heath's industrial relations tensions.

At that time, just yards to the railway and up over the Ed-wardian mansions, was the famous Wembley Stadium which I only got a good view of from beneath when we went to the market. Dad would say, 'You have no business in there,' especially on FA Cup Final Day when Wembley was in complete lockdown as many businesses, including shops, would close and buses were diverted.

My job at home was to take care of Fidel before and after school from the time he started school at age four. The worst time would be when Mum left for work and I had to brush his tough knotted hair. Mum used to call it 'African hair' and she didn't mean it as a compliment, singing out, 'Boy, where did you get this tough hair?' which would make Fidel cry out with every stroke of the comb. Sometimes the needles of the comb would break or it would snap in two. Because Fidel had a squint and his stock reply was always either 'No,' or he would say nothing, Mum would give me his tasks to complete, saying something light like, 'Make sure Fidel reads today. I put the books on the kitchen table.'

But I wanted to play, to relax, not have a younger brother cramp my style. Well, I might have thought that but would never say it. And sometimes, 'OK,' was just a tacit signal to my mother that I wasn't happy. I thought it was blindingly obvious that I wasn't happy. I was always crying and yet despite my mother's impatient, 'What's the matter?' her question seemed to make matters worse, so I'd cry even more.

That was it. Mum would be off to work. She used to wear a gingham coat with oval herringbone buttons that I would watch her delicate fingers do up, from top to bottom, never the other way. She would take her shopping bag in case she needed to purchase a multi-coloured scarf and she would wear her sensible grey or black shoes depending on the season … then she'd quickly check her purse to see if she had enough money and house keys and … out the door.

My heart would sink. At holiday time I would think *What will I do all day?* She would have already packed a lunch for us, made from ingredients I took out of the fridge for her. My primary concern was not to be noticed by strangers, so in summer we were dressed in unremarkable T-shirts, shorts and light running shoes. I had become self-conscious of my skin colour from hearing taunts in the school playground. Would people taunt us now? Even out with my mother, I'd worry. *How will I defend Mummy if I'm with her when there are taunts?* I thought. *Am I big enough and strong enough to do that? But why would people bother us?* I didn't understand because I reasoned that I wouldn't have done it to them. The world outside our secure home environment seemed a dangerous and strange place – no place for children.

On our own, we knew we could only go within a certain radius of the flat. Mum would tell us, 'Don't go near that slide'. I guess she had visions of Fidel sliding off and hurting himself. 'Don't go near the train tracks. I heard a rumour that someone …'

Still more chores to do … Mum did not have a tumble drier at home to dry clothes. Nor did a lot of my school friends' Mums, (though, granted, it wasn't a regular topic of discussion between us). But on a Saturday afternoon, I dreaded the words, 'Wilfred, can you take this washing to the laundry near the Town Hall?' And Mum would pack a shopping trolley with damp clothing for me to haul, and count out enough coins to cover two hours of drying.

'Yes Mummy,' I would dutifully reply, thinking this was a disaster. I had one treat and that was to take my comics on the fate of the Romans, which contained wild battles with grizzly endings. These would keep me occupied and stop me from slipping into boredom while the clothes from our home dried in a big steel metal drum with glass doors, so you could see when the clothes were dry. A woman sat in an office in the corner of the laundrette but I never spoke to her unless there was a problem. I'd pack the clothes back into the trolley and wheel it back home before it got dark. Mum would inspect the clothes and always seemed happy with the result, which was a blessing.

Chapter 26
Déjà vu

In the late summer leading up to September 1973 and just a few months before my twelfth birthday, I was due to start high school and I heard Mum and Dad discussing which school I would attend. It wasn't automatic that I would attend the local school, Copeland High Wembley, as it was notorious for its knife crime. So my parents settled on Neasden High. Mum told me we'd need to pay a visit to Myers for my school uniform.

By now educators had introduced 'streaming' and I was put into a 'special class' for two years.

The nightmare began on my first day, with all my fears left over from my first day at infants' school being repeated. This school was under renovation, with some buildings only half-finished.

Mum dropped me on the way to take Fidel to his school at Chalkhill. I sat and waited and waited then a man who looked like a reincarnation of the principal at my old school, Mr Stephens – but not so sick – turned up and said, 'Follow me!' 'Clunk, clunk,' went the sound of my shoes as we crossed the playground, with my eyes looking down, as I didn't know where we were going.

The next horrors were worse than physical torture. My

mind was drifting back to what Mum had told me an age before, about having to work ten times as hard as others due to racism. Yes, it looked and felt like racism to me, a shattering admission I made to myself. As an eleven-year-old boy, I just wanted to be left alone in peace, without people telling me what I was <u>not</u> – and telling me, not because they knew me but just because they could tell me. We slowly walked up a set of stairs and entered a new classroom filled with the noise and movement of kids, none of whom looked like me but all causing considerable disarray and not wearing full uniform. With dark skin and dressed in my uniform, I must have looked a right sight to them. All I could sense was oblivion, my dream of peace wiped away.

I just sat silently. It never occurred to me to protest. Who would listen anyway? All I could think about was the shame of telling my parents that I was now in the 'R' for 'Remedial' stream with a bunch of white working class kids who were being prepared for a lifetime of what? I sat near the back of the classroom where no one could see me unless they turned around. And why would they bother, I thought? Then I noticed through my tears a boy with tousled hair and a chalk-white face looking a little too hard into my gentle features. He maintained a stern look, almost of disapproval.

'What are you doing here?' he asked me.

'I really don't know.'

'Well, you don't belong here.'

'Yes, I know,' I replied, and started to cry, more from despair than from any real appreciation of my predicament. But I decided then to make the best of the situation at school from that day on.

In September 1975 I would begin studying for my O levels

and in mid-1978 I would take the exams – and fail most of them. I had to take them again in 1979. I passed and then entered the Lower Sixth from 1979 to 1981, leaving school at the age of nineteen, a year behind my original high school mates.

Chapter 27
Teenage summers

There was always anxiety for me about the summer holidays, lasting from late-July to early-September, because as a family, we never ever went away.

Dad was blunt saying, 'This is not my country I don't need to see any more. My holiday would be in my country of birth.' Dad could never be persuaded.

Every summer I would secretly hope he'd say, 'Let's go to the seaside'. I hadn't seen the sea. But instead of being taken to the seaside I became a 'latchkey child' during the school holidays. It was an open secret that a lot of kids were latchkey kids and during the summer holidays they were 'left up to their own devices'. So long as they didn't maim, kill or steal, that was considered alright.

By early high school, my holiday activities consisted of taking Fidel and Herman to a play area with a slippery slide on top of a hill. The slide was made of silvery metal and was steep, and in case of an unfortunate event when you might lose control, you had to hold the sides, not too tightly, mind, as they were sharp. The park had tall poplars that seemed to touch the clouds.

Then there was a paddling/swimming pool in the form of

a snake and this was a treat for the children, but only toddlers and younger kids could paddle and frolic. You could hear laughter all the way to our block of flats thirty metres away. The funny thing was the pool was never complete; either the water pump didn't work or someone would leave shards of glass in the bottom of the pool. So much for community recreation during the holidays!

On Sundays it was customary for our family to visit friends in another part of London. It appeared to me that it was a mark of respect if you visited them rather than receive them at your own home. There was no explanation from either of my parents as to why we visited these people but I came to realise there was a strong connection between Dad and Mum and Shafik and Toni, as they were all from Trinidad, and even the same town, Tunapuna. I picked up from conversation between the adults that they knew each other's parents, siblings and friends. This was alien to me as I thought I didn't have a connection to them. They were the first and only non-family members who I gradually came close to.

Fidel and I would know that a visit to Shafik and Toni was due as Mum would give us instructions in advance about what was to occur. Mum would explain how we would travel there, what food to accept or not and that we were not to speak out unless spoken to, nor get up without permission and wander around their house. I would think, *Why all these rules and restrictions?* It really irritated me but I accepted it as the price of getting out of our flat and going to another part of London. Though Mum said we could play with their children, this never really took off as they seemed to be under the same restrictions as us. I don't know what Fidel thought as he seemed disinterested. I thought Toni's name sounded like a boy's name but then I would reason that she was a woman. I didn't have the courage to ask Mum about the conundrum.

This family was special to ours because we didn't visit anyone else on a Sunday, not even Auntie and Uncle. Shafik and Toni lived in Edmonton. We'd set out late morning from home, travelling by underground train and then bus. I would scream to myself that this was taking forever as I kept an eagle eye on Fidel. That was my job. I knew Dad and Mum would have much to say if there was a problem with Fidel. He disliked holding my hand and seemed inclined to do the very thing that Mum hated the most in a child, to 'drag' – that is, walk at a very slow pace and fall behind the adults so that then Mum would drag him along, creating a scene in the street.

It was a relief when we'd finally arrive at the door, always answered by the man of the house, Shafik, a short fellow with a big belly and dark hair, resembling a dog with a sad look on his face. He would greet Dad with 'How you doin', boy?' and Dad would reply, 'Not bad. And yourself?' – and so it would go. He seemed similar in some ways to Dad, for instance he could seem frightening! Toni was taller than Mum, and had skin that to me appeared white, with brown hair that was straight. She seemed very lively, even excitable, and struck me as someone to keep well away from, but there was no escape as she leant down to kiss me on my cheek. That revolted me but I could say and do nothing, given Mum's instructions. Toni would greet Mum, smiling and laughing, with, 'Girl, you seem to have put on a bit of weight! When is the next one due?' Mum would giggle and I would see her in a different light. Gone was the restriction, and a lighter, more bubbly person would emerge. I enjoyed it while it lasted as there'd be none of that when we got back to Chalkhill later that evening.

Their front room was like ours: a big cabinet full of glass and china, a dining table with four dark wooden chairs. The room was carpeted. Toni and Mum would disappear into the kitchen and, sitting with Fidel and making sure he didn't make a run for it, I would try not to fall asleep, Toni's children also having slipped away from us. I felt abandoned, gazing at Dad and Shafik talking quietly but confidently to each other, oblivious to my turmoil. I felt a real dislike of adults sometimes as they concentrated on themselves and this was one of those times. Most of their conversation related to 'back home'. *Strange*, I thought. *Isn't London home?* It seemed not.

The conference between Shafik and Dad would be abruptly interrupted with an announcement that dinner was ready, which always pleased me. I thought we'd eat Trinidadian food, and wasn't disappointed. There was salad, goat and chicken curry, callaloo (spinach) and Indian roti, all steaming hot and placed on the dining table. The only non-Trinidadian dish was a huge English trifle. I could smell the rum in it without even seeing it, my mouth watering at the prospect of a huge slab of red jelly, soft sponge base, rich white cream and 'hundreds and thousands' liberally sprinkled on top. That to me made up for all the adults' faults.

After that big lunch I would fall asleep and wake to hear the adults talking quickly, laughing and smiling at each other. I would be glad when Dad would announce, 'Well, it's getting late. We should be on our way, Shafik.' 'Yes, boy,' he'd say. 'Don't let the cold catch you out.' And they'd both laugh. I didn't get the joke. Mum and Toni would look at the men with dislike. Then it was hats and coats and we were gone until the next Sunday.

So these visits seemed to constitute the major part of my

school holiday activities. In any case, by 1974, I had become more and more interested in Labour politics, to the extent I was thinking of myself as a boy politician. It was hard to ignore the injustices I would hear about on radio and television, and read about in newspapers. This year clearly marked my burgeoning interest in politics, with a series of major events in the national news: the three-day miners' strike, continuing troubles in Northern Ireland and the settling-in period of Britain's entry into the EEC. As well as the early years of the rise of the despicable National Front.

Chapter 28
My musical and political education

By 1975 I was still listening to the radio a lot as an outside channel for ideas and cultural experience, soaking up what I could draw into my confined life. I felt a particular excitement when I'd turn on my transistor radio – exerting a sense of freedom of choice. The music of Marc Bolan, the Bay City Rollers and Rod Stewart was an integral part of breakfast radio, and I began developing my own vinyl collection. I'd go back to Kilburn and use my pocket money to buy albums, and Mum had also given me a small record player which became my pride and joy. I used to jump on Fidel if he so much as breathed on it. I had a fondness for playing it with the volume turned up.

I knew my parents had an interest in Trinidadian music, specifically Calypso with its rhyming tradition. Dad would have Mum in stiches when it came to some of the old time Lord Kitchener and steel pan music, which Dad was proud to say was the only instrument invented in the 20th century. The music was created from beating on old oil drums, as Dad explained. Mum and Dad also liked jazz, which was not really 'my cup of tea'. At school we talked about the latest boy bands, and I would secretly fantasise about the lead male singers of the Bay City Rollers or Marc Bolan, with his flowing straight hair, open shirt exposing his chest, wide flared trousers and the best of all platform shoes. Mum said I could buy a pair. They very much resembled the building blocks I used to put together.

Adolescence was creeping up on me. When I turned thirteen, Dad pointed out that I had hair under my arms and on my face. Mum made no comment.

So 1975 was the year puberty really hit. Dad's contribution was to ask me how it felt. Well, it felt embarrassing to be asked. I would get hot in the face and cast my face towards the ground with an embarrassed smile, which I hoped would prevent any more questions.

'Do you need to shave?' he asked me. But I couldn't look at myself in the mirror, thinking I was so black and ugly, with a big nose and ears. I'd sneak a glance and then look away.

Being in the lowest academic stream didn't help my self-esteem, nor the anodyne school where teachers used a word I came to hate, 'conscientious' – which to me, reading between the lines, meant 'tries hard but is dull'. That was so not me. But I continued to strive.

The word 'puberty' felt very unconnected to me. It sounded very formal. I would examine the sprouting hair all over my body, on my face with my very oily skin and the spots that went with it, and under my arms and around my genitals. I was daily waiting for the terror that was my voice dropping …

Three years later when I turned sixteen I was allowed to stay up later, and one evening when Dad got home from work, he asked me some preliminary questions, and poured Danish lager into a glass and left the can there for me to see. Then to my surprise he left the room. I had a sip of the glass and immediately headed to the fridge, opened a blackcurrant juice and poured some in, making a ghastly mixture. It was more palatable to drink, I thought, and Dad caught me doing this and was confused. Had I done something wrong by drinking the lager? Dad's eyes were all that spoke initially, as if inspecting the outcome of an experiment. Eventually, to my relief, he said, 'So you didn't like it then?' I was so hesitant to say anything that might offend him, I stayed silent for a while. Then with my stomach tightening, I said with a weak smile, 'No, I didn't like it'. 'OK,' he said – and we never spoke of alcohol again.

Also when aged sixteen, I heard Dad say, 'You're old enough to visit Trinidad. Would you like to go with me?' My head spun. I gave no answer, just put my head down, as Dad watched, his penetrating gaze intimidating. I felt it gave me no place to hide. I had an urge to say no, but felt nothing about a place I couldn't imagine even though Dad had talked incessantly about Trinidad for as long as I could remember. I thought it would be nice if Mum could come, but that just remained a thought. They had probably discussed and agreed that Dad would go with me on this occasion. I hoped there would be time for Mum and me to travel together.

'OK, Dad, I would like to go with you in August.'

Mum asked me if I'd like to come with her and spend part of the summer holiday where she worked. This was something I really did want to do, to be close to Mum at St Mary's Hospital, where I'd read the women's magazines after having been introduced to her boss, Professor Ward. Usually I didn't meet strangers eye-to-eye but I did meet him, and he would talk to me about school and my love of history.

So I ended up both spending some time at my mother's workplace and going to Trinidad. But that came later. Back when I was thirteen, in the August 1975 school holidays, I spent most of my time with Fidel and Herman down by the railway track looking for foxes. That seemed the safest thing to do.

In my home setting, my growing interest in history and politics seemed to be a natural fit as Dad would argue vociferously at the TV, Mum or me. There was plenty to interest me in a Labour government. I would listen, burning with desire to find a space to speak. Dad bought two newspapers a day and I would listen to the Home Service on BBC Radio.

In doing my reading homework, I became fuelled by English Lit, and a teacher called Mr Edwards who was big, broad and never ever smiled or revealed anything of his character. He was so unlike another teacher who seemed positively risqué and passionate in discussions. I used to look at this teacher's backside but decided my thoughts were best left unspoken. I did find some school friends attractive and would give any excuse to be near one close friend. I would even pick a fight just so I could touch him. But he told me clearly he was going to marry and have kids. Still … I could hope. At least in Rugby I could eye boys – but I heard that the other boys were involved in sex with girls. I didn't really believe a lot of what was said and, anyway, a deputy head boy, as I would become, had to be seen to be above that.

It was decided my brother Fidel would go to Neasden High. I groaned. Responsible for my brothers at home and now for Fidel at school as well – it felt too much of a burden. Herman was starting school at St Joseph's Infant's. Fidel had become sullen and Herman hyper active. I had to make sure I collected Herman on time so I couldn't take longer than expected in the afternoon – although there were some shortcuts by train, and Herman would threaten me, 'I will tell Mummy what you did.'

And sure enough, he did.

Some mornings I would get up with a heavy sense of dread. I hoped against hope that things would improve for me. But I didn't know, from age eleven on, how I could make a difference to have adults see me with all my passion. My silence was passive resistance against what had been done to me without justification. Too often my disappointment with teachers or my parents presented itself as silence. I was desperate to say what I felt but I never felt safe enough to speak. Never. I would walk downstairs in the morning knowing my parents had gone through difficulties in choosing that high school for me but I came to resent it. It was tangled emotion I felt, mixed with a fierce and unarticulated love. Yes, love – when I didn't even yet know the meaning of the word.

The school subjects I looked forward to were at first principally craftwork and woodwork. I loved the feel and smell of grey lumps of clay, and working wood with my hands. Our teacher, Mr Twigg, was from Liverpool, wore a cravat and walked around in florid shirts and with crazy hair that seemed to imitate the long dead Marc Bolan who, shock horror, had a black girlfriend who died in a driving accident when a car ploughed into a tree.

I took in all the lessons tentatively, keeping my head down, looking for an escape route to more academic classes. *Surely they'll see the mistake they made and let me move up a class*, I would tell myself. But it was out of my hands and I knew it. Painfully aware of being in the academic slow train, I felt abandoned, feeling that a 'not understood future' was at stake. But I had a burning determination to right what I saw as a wrong associated with the colour of my skin.

I was terribly shy about expressing what I was thinking

but decided in the summer of 1974, despite being in the lower stream, to get up in front of the whole morning assembly to read a passage from the Bible. My soul had spoken to me: 'If you don't speak up, no one will ever hear you or know that you existed'. The reading was accompanied by a piece of classical music, that morning a Rachmaninov concerto. As I finished the reading, I felt a great sense of relief and freedom.

My school reports mirrored the reports I'd received at Fryent: 'Tries hard, must try harder. Conscientious,' which to my developing intuition meant 'Dull but just doesn't know it'. Or 'A fool'. *I will show them*, I thought, taking a line from Mum about 'Doubting Thomases', even though I still didn't know what it meant.

At Chalkhill we only had two bedrooms so, with three children, things were getting tight. Mum put in for an accommodation transfer with Brent Council but she said, 'Who knows how long we'll wait?' Mum looked at one property and gave a deposit but came home very angry about rat infestation and dirty rising damp. Dad told her the agent was a crook and she needed to get her money back. I listened to this and very much wanted to go with her if Dad wasn't going. But I never asked. Mum said, 'He's not going to get away with this,' and that was that. I imagined what the East End must have been like, and then she arrived back with the money. I was so proud of Mum but didn't say it. I just watched her tell the story of her success.

One day Mum was angry and I heard her say, 'We were never slaves!'

I asked, 'What do you mean?'

What was my own ambition in life? Well, I'd moved on from fireman to Prime Minister but when I expressed that idea to one friend, he backed away as if I'd just farted, and I burned up inside. When would people take me seriously? I hunted for books in the library about black people, any black people. But I couldn't find one, not one.

Meanwhile my daily walks to and from school on the bridge over the swift-running River Brent seemed regularly to invite salacious goings-on between my school mates and girls from the local school. Drinking, smoking, sex – none of that interested me.

By 1977 to 1978, I was getting ready for exams. I had an interest in Economics, History and Geography and was still really keen on English Lit and craft-based subjects. In 1978, one teacher, Mr Cox, who was in his mid-twenties, used to give me an odd stare. An Oxford PPE, he was a short, wiry man with an intense gaze. I think I fell in love with his intellectual gifts. He taught me Economics Essays in the Lower Sixth.

In 1978 I thought the focus on 'black boys' at school was generally negative. Teachers made the final selections about which exams all the boys would sit. The black boys were mostly always chosen for the non-academic exams, and I was one of the few who were allowed to sit for academic exams, with the ultimate goal of going to university. So I was disappointed when some boys would fall into the stereotypes that had been set up for them. One friend, for instance, used to expose himself to amuse his friends. One technical drawing teacher, Mr Braddon, who was in his eighties, used to move so very slowly that he couldn't see what was going on. Then we'd all get into trouble. I'd tell my friend to 'put it away' because I thought he was letting us all down, as 'black boys'.

Miss Gousseff was one of my History teachers. A thin wiry woman, she had a persistent cough and did not have much confidence in my intellectual gifts, so I always doubted myself even though I loved History.

To get into the Sixth Form you had to pass 5 O Levels at a certain grade. When it came to school subject choices, I enjoyed Art and Craft classes such as Pottery and Woodwork. As for sport, I had my finger in every pie that was available, be it athletics, basketball or rugby.

So at first I hid the subject choice form I'd brought home from school, but finally I had to show it to Dad. He came into my room and stood over me as I sat at my desk and he told me I was going to do Economics, Geography and History and that no son of his would be working with his hands.

What I really didn't like about him was that we never did father-and-son things. He was always telling, telling, telling – never simply showing. For example, despite Dad's challenging views about religion, I really enjoyed stories about Christ's crucifixion. At one point I even wanted to be a priest.

Mum's stories were also sustained, but she would tell hers when Dad wasn't around to contradict her. It was always difficult for her to talk when he was at home, and I often wanted to tell Dad to shut up and let Mum speak – which I did once when they were arguing. I took her side and Dad turned on me ferociously, telling me to mind my own business and never interfere again. I glared at him, with tears welling up in my eyes. I could hit him for the way he treated Mum, but I simmered down, dimly realising that he might be right, though I hated to admit it. The experience left me shaken as it was the first time I'd confronted Dad. I decided it would be easier to do what he had advised me to do: walk quietly with a big stick. I also remember him telling me, 'What she went through to look after you! But you were always a good boy. She had to hustle from home to work, getting you to the child-minder on the way, and making her way through snow and ice.'

I seemed to count the hours and days when I'd be free of school. But what was beyond the walls of school and home? As my understanding and reasoning grew, I had to appreciate the error of my ways at secondary school. What emerged was a riotous carnival of suffering the like of which I imagined had not been witnessed in the northern hemisphere for some time. A universe that had people that were *coloured.*

I kept a thin blue diary but my interest in boys was left as a secret so Mum couldn't snoop. But I did express my ardent interest in a Greek Cypriot boy. Mostly I wrote stuff about the weather – good days and bad days. Test results. Arguments with friends. There were entries on 'Ice skating today' and 'Have my own pocket money'.

I also wrote some entries about Mark, a boy with cystic fibrosis, who was tall, with paper-thin white skin and protruding front teeth. Lots of knees and elbows. I disliked him on sight. Yet he wanted to be friends with me and I felt sorry for him. We would meet in the school playground and he'd chat about his model planes and cars. I would listen, trying not to look at his face which left me feeling sick. I didn't know why, but I noticed none of my friends wanted to have anything to do with him either.

My friends even bullied him sometimes. He died when I was about fifteen and it was my first experience of a friend dying. I felt ambivalent about it. I was sad but knew he was now out of his misery of ill-health. I was also surprised that the friends who had bullied him were visibly upset and I wondered whether they felt guilty.

Chapter 29
Racism and results at school

Parents Open Evenings were when parents, their children and teachers would meet to discuss their child's progress over the previous year. The sessions would be held at the end of the school day. A couple of weeks before the meetings, we'd be issued with our yearly school reports. These would cover each subject area studied, with comments from your subject teacher about your progress and a grade attached. The school reports were also a reflection of how exam ready you were.

On that first evening, the first teacher Dad wanted to see was Miss Tasker, my English teacher who was Head of Department. Her name was on the half-open door and the room was flooded with light. As we entered, I noticed there was no one else waiting to see her. I was dreading the meeting as I had had previous form in poor yearly reports and general performance at school for as long as I could remember.

We drew up two chairs and sat in front of Miss Tasker who had her back to the classroom window. She said she was from the Midlands. She was tall and slim with blond hair, had youthful white skin and spoke confidently.

With the pleasantries out of the way, Dad did not waste time in pointing out Miss Tasker's teaching faults to her. Dad had brought what he called my English copy book, a Trinidadian word for the school exercise book. I knew what was coming, given how Dad would question everything that had been marked. 'These teachers can't teach,' he'd tell me at home, with me mute as this didn't seem to be a battle I could ever win, even if I could put an argument. I kept listening as he spoke to Miss Tasker but there was nothing for me to say; it was as if I wasn't there. I thought perhaps she deserved what Dad was dishing up to her. I stole a glance at Dad's face and saw he didn't hesitate and spoke clearly.

Dad took out of his bag the book which she had marked with a C+ and approving comments. When I saw Dad had done that I wondered, *What next?* My heart sank as he spoke.

'How could you mark this as correct when clearly he has misspelled this and this?' Dad's fingers pointed relentlessly at every page error. Miss stuttered and stammered. It must have been a rare experience for her, one she'd never let me forget. She really said nothing to refute his accusations. His questions and her red face stammering seemed to go on without end. Then it was over and we stood to go. Dad and Miss Tasker shook hands and it was all done for another year.

The next day arriving at school, I had even greater dread about what awaited me. Yet when I took Miss Tasker's class she made no comment and her attitude towards me hadn't changed. I wondered if this was too good to be true. Miss Tasker was, on past evidence, never one to let a slight go unanswered. I would just have to be more vigilant than ever and wait and see what happened in the future.

A few days before another parents' night at school, Dad had told me there were enough black boys in sports and he didn't need for me to join them. Come the night, the sports teacher, Mr Davidson, his bald pate shining, took on an air of extra menace, his jaw set. He was always dressed in a track suit, seeming to me as if he was perpetually immediately ready for some sporting activity. He sat at his desk, all testosterone, and as bald as a ball in snooker, the only game Dad loved to play. Whereas I was good at all sports except tennis. I loved rugby especially. As I sat there watching my father and Mr Davidson, I had an oppressive sense I would never be able to play to my potential. I sensed Dad was angry. They shook hands, no smiles, just looking at each other. Did I imagine aged just fourteen that there was a struggle taking place and that it was over whose son I was, and what would become of me. This was not something I wanted to think, not at all, but there it was. It held my attention while Mr Davidson and Dad spoke about all things sport. I don't think Mr Davidson knew what had hit Dad when suddenly he said, 'Well, I see Wilfred is down for a lot of sport activities. I appreciate all your support for my son, but from next term he won't be playing again.'

The classroom was empty except for these two adversaries. I was aware of just the lights being on and occasional footsteps and whispered conversations between parents and children in the corridor.

Mr Davidson had been silenced for a moment.

'I don't think you realise how talented your son is,' he said.

Dad cut him off. 'Yes, I know that. And that's why his parents have decided that he should not do any more sport.'

Mr Davidson went red in face. *It's funny*, I thought, *that Europeans' emotions can show so obviously due to their skin colour, whereas you have to look very hard to find out what I'm thinking behind my complexion*. I could conceal my feelings and it became a habit. I knew I would suffer not being allowed to play sport but that was Dad. Once his mind was made up, that was an end to it.

These incidents were puzzling enough, but the confusion I felt over the everyday judgements made about me by teachers, and taunts from other children, was an even heavier emotional load to carry.

One morning in March 1975, two years after having been assigned to a remedial class, a teacher told me to come to another classroom with him, which I did with a falling heart. Could there be an even lower class I was being taken to, I wondered? We arrived outside a wooden door in the science block. We went in and I tried to catch a glimpse of who was in the room. It turned out to be my least favourite class: Arithmetic, which I hated with a passion. Then, in full glare of a crucifix around the female teacher's neck, I saw thirty faces stare back at me. They knew where I had come from, the dunces' class, and surprise surprise, I reproached myself bitterly. I was black. I felt a pain rise up in my chest as if I could at that moment take a dagger and stab the teachers. The teacher who'd brought me over to the new class left the room without so much as a glance at me. *Bastard*, I thought. I was one that got away! Then I remembered that he was rumoured to be having an affair with another teacher. *Can teachers ever be trusted?* I thought. They disgusted me but I feared what they could do to my mind, and what life prospects I had. Find a seat anywhere, the teacher with the cross told me. I looked around, bewildered and embarrassed.

Then, like a shining angel appearing in the midst of a very dark place, a voice said, clear and loving, 'Why don't you come and sit next to me?'

Who was this beacon of hope? I turned to my left and saw

a spotty but handsome-faced boy with hair like mine. I could see he was taller than me, and was wearing a neat school uniform and looked somewhat like me. He smiled at me and I returned the favour with relief, walking across to him as smartly as I could. He had spoken with an accent I didn't recognise, which I found out later was Guyanese, and from that moment we became firm friends.

The fact was that despite my sense of shame, I'd been elevated to a higher class, so I told my parents about this success when I got home.

Dad said, 'Well done, son,' and Mum said, 'I have cooked dinner for you.' My brothers were understandably indifferent.

But given the previous experience at Neasden – from my very first day in September 1973 and how I'd been treated ever since then – I still felt angry and confused about the way I'd been taken out of remedial class and dumped in a strange classroom without any explanation. *What will it take for me to be treated fairly, regardless of my skin colour?* I wondered.

There were other incidents of a racial nature concerning school work when I felt unfairly picked on by teachers. Once after a particularly hard day at school with certain teachers making my life difficult for no better reason I could see than that my skin was darker than theirs, I decided to raise the problem at home. Instead of telling Mum about it, I thought – given my age – that Dad might be sympathetic.

He heard me out but did not address my complaint. He simply said, 'We can't protect you while you're at school. You'll have to figure that out for yourself.' He said it without a tinge of sympathy. Racism was never a subject of conversation initiated by me.

But I was left feeling enraged at the unfairness of the situation and the fact that even my own father was not prepared to help. I vowed to myself that no mention of such incidents of a racial nature involving me would be reported to Dad. I would sort things out by myself as the only person to be relied on was me.

Chapter 30
Adolescent angst

Sometime during my senior years at school, I decided that my true inclination was that I was interested in men, and that became a factor in my considerations about my future. I felt that if I hadn't realised it already in my life so far, my life ahead was never going to be easy.

Yet I resolved to be the best possible person I could be without 'losing myself'. I was under no illusions. The new school year would bring exam challenges and I wondered if I was avoiding responsibility in my lack of preparation for the exams. I needed five O Levels at C or above to get into the Sixth Form. My closest friends had been studying hard so I should do it too. I knew what subjects I wanted to study at A Level, yet the harder I burned the midnight oil the more elusive that prize seemed.

When at last I reached Sixth Form at age sixteen in 1978, I was approached by the deputy headmaster to ask whether I wanted to be deputy head prefect. I got the feeling that I should feel grateful to accept the position – but I thought I was popular enough to be the head prefect, not the deputy. I agonised about the decision, thinking that it was some vindication yet also thinking that there was still some element of racism in offering me the second-best position. Finally, I accepted it.

My Dad seemed rarely to hold any teacher in high regard but this did not apply to the head teacher of Neasden High School, Mr Luke Nesbitt, who seemed to me from another age. Mr Nesbitt was short and rotund, with pale skin, topped off with a mop of grey hair. He wore clothing that seemed straight out of the 19th century and had a deep bass voice that could penetrate any corner of the school. Every day he wore a white shirt, a tie with the School crest, a black gown that flapped about when he moved at speed through the school. polished black shoes that shone and were pointed at the tip of the toe, and his feet splayed out. He resembled a waddling duck when he walked, white shirt, tie and gown flapping about him when, as often was the case, he moved about the school on the lookout for miscreants. My school friends nicknamed him 'The Joker' after the character in the Batman movies. We kept this 'joke' to ourselves, as Mr Nesbitt did not appear to have a sense of humour.

I never counted myself among the band of naughty boys as I knew this just wouldn't work for me. I understood that if I got into trouble then I would be another statistic of a black boy headed for the scrap heap. I kept telling myself every day that I needed to get 5 O Levels not CSEs to get into the Sixth Form to be able to study at Advanced Level. Our school teachers, who were predominantly white, would not hesitate to put black boys such as myself and my friend Derek into 'easier' non-academic classes which would lead straight out of the school gate at the minimum school leaving age of sixteen.

I think one of the reasons Dad liked Mr Nesbitt was that he ran a tight ship. All the teachers understood who was in charge. The pupils knew it too. He also had a close relationship with the Education Department as well as Government Ministers in Mrs Thatcher's first government. Our teachers would alert us when a dignitary arrived at school, trailing behind Mr Nesbitt's gown. It was a sight to behold and a source of much sniggering when Mr Nesbitt was out of sight. He had presence which could chill your blood; he seemed to know what you were thinking and he'd fix you with a stare.

If you had the misfortune to be reported to the headmaster's office, you were most likely to be caned. It was the case that boys would receive the cane and girls would receive their punishment with a couple of strokes of a ruler. I had heard from school friends who had had to wait outside Mr Nesbitt's office, that he had a formidable array of canes which, depending on the seriousness of the infringement, would be administered by him on the backside or hands. Some school friends told me caning the hands was the worst punishment in that the pain lingered long after the blow. Students might also receive detention after school or be reported at home.

I understood early on that when it came to homework I was on my own. Once when I brought French school work home, Dad was reading the 'Daily Mirror' looking at the form, and hunched over the kitchen table. I waited silently, afraid for the first time to ask him for help, and then mustered the courage, standing right behind him.

'I can't do this …' My words trailed off and he didn't turn around. I felt aggrieved, realising he didn't care. He was very hard on me. After what seemed to be an eternity, he said, 'There is no such word as can't'. He refused to look at my homework book. That was it for me. I never touched or spoke French again.

When I listened to Dad on a Sunday afternoon and he

touched on schooling, he seemed to be proud of the schooling he'd received. But the discipline and corporal punishment seemed very severe to me. Dad told me that schooling in his day was harsh. If you got a place at the government school there was punishment with a belt, dished out for lateness or talking or not being able to recite something from memory. It seemed as if you could be beaten for anything. He didn't have a school uniform and went to school in bare feet. Yet he felt he was living in an idyll as there was no television or radio, but there were newspapers. Literacy levels were low and men would gather around as the latest court cases were read out loud. Since you could be hanged for murder, the reports excited interest.

Knowing the conditions Dad had gone through, I knew there was little point in complaining about my school's homework demands. I had opportunities others didn't and I had to make the best of them.

Chapter 31
To 'Paradise' and back

In that summer of 1978, sitting with Dad in our front room when he unexpectedly asked me, 'Would you like to visit Trinidad?' my mind was a mixed bag. Just sixteen, having taken my O Levels and some CSE subjects, I was now waiting for the results.

'Trinidad?' What did that mean? Flying across the world to meet my paternal grandmother and maternal grandfather. *All too much*, I thought at first. *But then, it would beat an English summer. My friends are going away. Well, this would be a tale to tell.* I said yes, and we were gone a month.

Before we left, I examined our atlas to find the speck that I called, 'Trinidad and T…'

'No …' Dad said, '… no Tobago. You were born in Trinidad!' This was said with such vehemence that I remembered in Dad's hearing in future always to say 'Trinidad' and not 'Trinidad and Tobago', even though that was the official name of the country.

I experienced my first earthquake; milked the last cow of my grandfather's herd; saw the fields of tall luscious cane sugar he grew; met some of my mother's sisters, fat and thin; saw fireflies for the first time in the still, quiet heat of the tropical evenings; went up to Caura where Dad and Auntie Carmen had grown up, a town now overtaken by the forest reclaiming it. I marvelled that light shone through the forest canopy in perfectly round holes. I was wary of snakes after Dad's sermons about sitting on rocks that turned out to be poisonous snakes. I saw forest wild cats, jaguar and strange coloured birds. The capital, Pos, where I was born, looked grimy and chaotic around all the major landmarks. We took gifts from Mum for her Dad, sisters, brothers, nieces, nephews and cousins, most of whom called me English on account of my accent, my clothes and my restrained behaviour. In other words, not loud like them.

What had I agreed to? Being away from Mum and my brothers for the first time ever. Dad telling me what was possible and what was not. The trip became a confusing jumble in my head. In some ways I even wanted to get it over and done with.

'Dad, there's no hot water!' Yes, I did get used to that common situation. I found I had a lot to learn.

I meet my paternal grandmother for the first time. She knew me as a baby. Although she has dementia she is cared for by Catholic nuns.

I meet my maternal grandfather for the first time since 1962 when I was a newborn. He is tall, dark as night, with gnarled hands like an English oak tree. I remember what I regard as fantastical stories told by Mum of how she worked from the age of six, while he went to the Panama Canal and was kept in chains but somehow managed to escape.

He never directly looks me in the eye, probably because he hardly knows me. But he is happy as we progress through the streets of Tunapuna. People refer to him by his nickname, *Clarky,* and it is a great thing for him to say with obvious pride,

'This is my grandson who left for England as a baby, and look at him now – a big, strong handsome boy!' At which point, I look away in embarrassment.

I also meet Dad's oldest sibling, living in an old house. He is eccentric, with chickens running in and out of the place. He barely eats yet insists on giving my father and me a ring each.

I can see there are positives and negatives to a life limited to this tropical paradise.

Chapter 32
Teenage privacy

Back home in London, what was looming were choices to be made about the subjects for O Levels and CSEs. My heart went with craft subjects but Dad would say, 'No. We don't want any more black men working with their hands,' echoing his statement of a few years before that there were enough black men in sport. Essentially, his argument was that we needed more intellectuals – doctors, teachers, managers, just as he was a manager. I was awed by Daddy's intellect. Mum did not appear in any of these conversations and I wished she would. They were just between Dad and me, and it was an unequal contest as I didn't have the verbal skills to counter Dad's arguments. All I had was frustration and tears. Nor could I draw on my friends as Dad didn't know my friends. I couldn't invite them to my home after the debacle of having invited one white friend and then cancelled because I was embarrassed about him. I realised I would just have to wait until I left school to live my life the way I wanted, and have whatever friends I liked round to my place, including gay men.

After my Trinidad holiday, our family moved again in 1979, to 49 Runbury Circle, Kingsbury. As I matured through my adolescence I would see clearer evidence of my parents' view of the world, for example Mum trying to persuade Dad to dress appropriately and Dad insisting that he was 'King of my own Castle'. In summer he would dress in a string vest and his underwear, and in the winter he'd wear trousers, shirt and jumper.

'I have only worn a tie once, and that was on my wedding day,' he would tell me. Mum would 'um' and 'ah' to no effect. Yet she too had her uniform: a beige raincoat, hat and bag, and sensible shoes. She always had a kind word for anyone she met and had plenty of friends.

My parents lived by their own cultural standards as far as possible despite being embedded into the lowest levels of a white class-bound Anglo-Saxon society.

At 49 Runbury Circle, I used to love to do homework listening to Radio 4 until late, and also offshore and onshore pirate radio stations. I loved listening to plays and wanted to be on radio myself one day. I didn't go out, except to attend school discos.

My reason for staying home so much? I have a waking nightmare. *Perhaps it's true*, I tell myself, *perhaps I am an imposter*. Just like a white boy once said to me: 'Who do you think you are? You're a nobody. You're just a nobody.' I had to run for my life, leaving a disguise to outfox my interrogators. I had survived but knew, in the tough terrain called 'secondary school', that I had to be watchful of pitfalls prepared for me. These white boys were just a different shade of colour to me, I reasoned. But in the safety of his superiority, that white boy had spat out the words that marked me as an imposter. I wondered if it was true, in that moment when my solar plexus registered the hatefulness of those words and then my brain caught up in feverish anger. My mouth opened but no words came.

So I continue to wonder whether I am an imposter. *Perhaps it's true,* I think. *I have failed my ancestors, my father. I have always been marked for failure.*

In those crucial early and adolescent years, the teachers never let me forget it. Yet still somehow I make it through.

The country was experiencing a profound economic and social crisis. The UK had its first woman leader of any main opposition party, the Conservatives. Jim Callaghan was the Labour Prime Minister from 1976 to 1979, heading a minority Labour government. I now followed politics incessantly, particularly since I'd turned 18 and could now vote. There were many debates in the Upper Sixth Form about neo-liberalism, socialism and communism, and the belief that the Cold War was still a present reality. As well, the Ulster conflict would periodically flare up in bomb attacks in London and other parts of the United Kingdom.

Life was in a kind of stasis. I continued to help Mummy with the shopping, cooking and in cleaning my own room. I loved it when the two of us could sit and chat over a cup of tea. Dad continued with his Sunday sessions but they were more or less different for me, as I wasn't really interested. I would still listen but without much ardour. I had a little voice telling me to find my own way.

'No sex.' Dad's words would echo in my mind. 'You never follow the crowd,' he said once. I guess he meant, 'You stay true to yourself.'

And then in 1980 I took a keen interest in the Campaign for Homosexual Equality. I thought my privacy was safe but Mum would steam open my letters about the Campaign, which had been sent to me by a gay man who lived around the corner.

I couldn't ever be seen with him, because my parents might have found out and would have been very upset.

One day I was seized with a white-cold terror when I came home and my mother called for me to come upstairs where she was in my bedroom. She was holding an opened package which I could see had a U.S. postmark. I was simultaneously happy that I'd received a reply to my enquiry about gay pornography, and enraged because Mum had found me out.

I cursed under my breath. *Is there no end to her interfering? Haven't I kept my end of the bargain; she must know that I like men.*

I was angry but had never had a confrontation with Mum, ever. I felt trapped and decided to make a run for it.

As I headed towards the stairs for the door, she followed, all guns blazing. 'So where did you get these from?' she yelled. Before I could attempt to answer her, she screamed again, 'I'm going to tell your father!'

Defiant, I shouted back. 'Well, you shouldn't have opened my letters. It's not right – the content is none of your business.' I was struck by my level of anger, and went on, 'Mummy, I don't want you opening my letters ever again.'

The novelty of my response temporarily silenced my angry mother. She said nothing more but gave me a withering glare and disappeared into her room. She never opened my letters again. I was torn. Part of me wanted her to know; the other part of me wanted to maintain the illusion. What I was vaguely aware of, after surreptitious research in the library, was that the legal age of consent in England was sixteen for heterosexual couples but had only been set at age twenty-one for gay men in 1967. I had no one else to talk to, no one to confide in, no one to lean on. I was becoming desperate.

On leaving school at the age of nineteen in 1981, I began to be more independent. Going to or coming home from college, I'd branch out to take a different bus or walk a different route, which I enjoyed.

I'd walk to Chamberlayne Road, considered one of the 'hippest' streets in London, passing the haunts of the past like 'The Black Prince' pub and St John's school, noticing that most of the corner shops had gone by this time. On to Kilburn High Road and then down Edgware Road until I reached Marble Arch. Then I could take a bus or walk around to Soho and down to Trafalgar Square or Piccadilly Circus, where there was an underground cinema. Or over to St Martin-in-the-Fields, where another cinema was situated, to see French Noir films. Or even go to Leicester Square to the Swiss Centre, a crude eyesore built in the 1950s, its saving grace being that it had a cinema.

I became obsessed about seeing French Noir films, which I knew as an extension of my childhood thrill when Mum took me to the movies. Ever since then I'd been enchanted by the silver screen. Those last couple of years at school I felt like an adult but knew I would be dependent on my parents for some time. But I still wanted to taste some freedom that had been denied me in neither leaving home nor being able to invite friends home. Just being able to get up and go out to the cinema was enthralling for me. I was tackling one dark cloud of self-loathing at a time in the hope that I would eventually conquer them all.

I'd also sometimes go to Bayswater not so much for ice skating, which I couldn't stand, but because it provided a different environment for me to enjoy. I wasn't interested in making new friends or finding a boyfriend as I was still adamant that I wouldn't become active sexually until I was twenty. My sexuality was something I kept to myself and I only shared the information with someone connected to the Campaign for Homosexual Equality. Even so, I was wary of him because I felt he was romantically interested in me and he lived so close, just around the corner in St Andrews Mansions, a mock Tudor house where most of the residents had an inflated view of their own importance. When I'd canvassed before elections, I could see how resistant they were to the idea of voting Labour.

There was also the fact that I was still at school and this was a major drawback. The Arithmetic teacher who wore a cross had always been a thorn in my side, and one day we had a confrontation and I had to re-sit my exam rather than start A Level Economic History with my beloved Mr Cox. The bitter fact for me was that once again I was alone. All alone. Boy, how I hated school with a passion! I believed that if the colour of my skin had been just a few shades lighter, I would have been allowed the marks needed to pass.

Humiliated, I didn't bother to tell my parents, until I absolutely had to, that I had to stay on at school until my 19th birthday to re-take my A Levels.

I took my A Level exams in June and July 1981 with the hope that I would get 3 A Levels to get into a university or polytechnic. Although I had visited both, my heart wasn't in it. The truth was that in my mind I was taking these exams for my parents and to prove the teacher with the wooden cross wrong. Well, I learnt that was never a sound basis to proceed in life. I failed all but one of the exams, getting an E for History which was a bare pass. Dad and Mum's reactions when I told them seemed phlegmatic but I wondered about their thwarted ambitions for me.

After all, Dad had wanted me to train as a lawyer. I'd gone as far as an interview at Central London Poly and endured one of the worst interviews ever imagined with an extremely dark Trinidadian barrister, who was was very bitter about life. He proceeded to pour that bitterness all over me, telling me my marks weren't good enough, until I fairly ran from that interview room, which seemed like a dungeon. I imagined all the walled-up characters who had ever had the misfortune to learn or teach there.

I was sick of education and this last experience confirmed my worst low expectations of teachers. They were able to take out their frustrations on hapless schoolkids like me and, for those who were racist, indulge their hatred. After sifting through higher education options after university and poly-technics, I found there were slim pickings, just colleges. I decided on Nene College in Northampton, East Midlands. I would be living away from home for the first time in my 19 years, and was happy at least with that decision, happy that I had managed to organise this by myself. I told Dad and Mum that I would complete a BTEC course in Business Studies at Nene College in Northampton, that would take three years to complete. I would commute to and from college. Then I started to feel homesick before I had even packed my case. I told myself it would work out but that voice of reason was very, very weak.

Chapter 33
Nene College and home again

On a cold frosty morning in October 1981, I set out to attend college in Northampton. I stood at the bus stop near Runbury Circle waiting to catch the 182 to North Wembley overground station, a huge black suitcase by my side. A car pulled up and out stepped two plain clothes policemen. I didn't know who they were at that stage, as they walked directly towards me, ignoring everyone else at the stop. I feared what was to come.

First they asked for my identification, and I was angry that they'd asked me for an ID yet didn't ask any of the white citizens near me. I felt exposed and realised I would have to take care in how I responded. I had a student rail pass with my photo and handed it over. Then they asked me where I was going and I told them Nene College.

'And what's in your suitcase?'

'Clothes.' I felt humiliated by this stage. They insisted I open it. I fumbled with the small lock and key, worried that I might miss the bus and then the train north. Once I'd opened my case, I had to bend down to go through my clothing, to prove there was nothing of a suspicious nature in there and that I was telling the truth.

I was rattled but continued my journey, apprehensive

about facing whatever life at Nene College would offer me.

I was actually starting late as my marks weren't good enough to be accepted into a university or a polytechnic so I'd had to settle for third best. The debate in my mind was that I was fed up with being a student, but unemployment was rising under Thatcher's government policies and my chances of getting a job as a young black person were slim. As I also didn't want to disappoint my parents who had wanted me to stay in education, I'd settled on Nene College.

Once I arrived in Northampton, I had to meet the landlord in an unfamiliar city and then find the college for the induction, all on the same day. It seemed a bit too hard.

When I met the landlord, I didn't quite trust him because a tenant who was leaving as I arrived told me I shouldn't move in because he was creepy and there were no locks on the bedroom doors. So I only stayed for about two months, during which time I got chilblains from the cold, and thereafter had to wrap up my hands for protection, which I hated. I also fell into a depression, not wanting to get out of bed.

When I met my Year Head, Mr Holland, I was infatuated, for he seemed to accept me and was very kind. He gave me the name and address of a landlady who had a cheap room to rent. When she opened the door to me, I was shocked. She was Ghanaian, and was dressed in a negligee with feathers. I stayed there for the duration of the course, always trying to ignore her invitations to 'come up to my room'. Meanwhile I wanted a man and couldn't find one for love or money in Northampton.

I didn't really understand what was expected of me as a student, to complete assignments and study for exams. People were friendly but not approachable so I didn't forge any close connections. One link I made was through the student newspaper which had an editor who was in his thirties and told me he was a 'perpetual student'. At least it was a bit of fun for me being on the editorial committee. I wrote a few articles and it was only in this sphere that I felt a part of student life.

After I failed the first year of the course, Mr Holland said it was a good thing because I needed to get out into the world and do what I wanted to do. He had me understand that I wasn't cut out for business administration. He told me I was my own worst enemy, bottling up all my angst over a sense of failure.

I spent every weekend back at my parents' place in London, catching the train and bus in all weathers, just so I could feel a sense of safety and certainty on arriving back home.

One Sunday evening about a month after I'd started at Nene College, I was at home in Kingsbury and looked out the window of my bedroom, and then went downstairs and looked through the front door window. I had an eerie feeling. The house was deathly silent and I had some intuition that my uncle was coming with bad news.

Dad and Mum were in the kitchen with the door shut and that was unusual. I stood at the door and listened but neither of them had much to say. It was beginning to irk me.

I felt a bit foolish but went back to the front door and saw the familiar figure of my uncle, tall and dark, silhouetted against the street lights. It was an unusual time for him to visit.

'Hello, Wilfred. Are your Mammy and Daddy here?' His manner was polite but solemn, which was unusual, because he was always laughing when he was with my parents. I took him into the kitchen. There was no laughter that night. Dad indicated with a nod of his head for me to leave. I was hurt and felt a flare of anger inside of me, leaving reluctantly. I was pissed off to have to leave the kitchen because I was almost an adult, now aged nineteen.

Uncle stayed in the kitchen for some time while I stood at the top of the landing trying to pick up any morsel of news, but no luck. Then I heard Dad call, 'Wilfred, could you come downstairs please?' to which I responded promptly, racing into the warm kitchen.

'Your uncle is leaving now.'

I said my goodbyes to Uncle, escorting him to the door, and he gave me a reluctant sort of hug before walking back to 40 Torbay Road the way he'd come. When I entered the kitchen, Mum seemed more upset than Dad, who spoke in a solemn tone.

'Your cousin Cyprian has killed Michelle. The children are safe and he's in hospital.'

I reeled from the shock. I had known Cyprian ever since I was a baby, had gone to his and Michelle's wedding, and he'd been my favourite cousin in the UK. Somehow I knew, without Dad giving details, that this was a 'murder', not an accident. I was unable to fathom why someone would do this, let alone someone who was a member of my family.

Mum started to cry a little. I stared at Dad who looked so out of sorts. Mum composed herself and said, 'Wilfred, can you make the tea?'

'Yes, of course, Mummy,' and I set about preparing the dining table for evening tea. I wondered how we'd get through this as a family.

I didn't know it at the time but the marriage had been under strain, with continuing violence and even a restraining order taken out against Cyprian by Michelle. The day before I heard the news, Cyprian had killed her from blows to the head with a hammer. Then he left the house, locking the door with their two babies left inside. He drove to a bridge, got out and jumped down onto a paved road below, intending to take his life. But he did not succeed. He was taken to hospital and later sent to a psychiatric hospital where he would spend ten years in a locked ward.

Our family did survive the horror of this murder. On weekends coming home from Nene College, I'd look forward to spending time with Mum, Dad and my brothers, after having endured the long train trip, then the red double decker bus ride along Wembley High Street almost to the door. I'd walk slowly up Birchen Grove to reach home and feel the warmth inside. *What a contrast with those early years at 40 Torbay Road and that little box room we lived in*, I would think. I felt a sense of fulfilment that my parents' struggle, and mine as a child, had created this loving home.

By the following year I'd finished with Nene College and had a serious conversation with my parents about my future. They told me, 'It was your decision to go to college and it's up to you to decide what you do next – but you'll always be loved by us here'.

I tried work in a timber yard but didn't like it. So what next?

'I want to be a community worker, Mum' I announced.

'What's that?'

'I don't really know, but when I find out I'll let you know.'

And we both burst out laughing.

After what had happened with my cousin I had a fear that I wouldn't be able to make anything of my life. But one day I saw an advertisement in an advice bureau for volunteers to work with people of Afro-Caribbean descent who were in psychiatric care.

So I went to a meeting – which coincidentally was back in Kilburn near my first home in England as an infant – and sat in a dark corner of the meeting room so I wouldn't be noticed. I had a clear intention that I would become Chair of the committee, raise money and organise volunteers. But I was shy. Then in response to the call for nominations, I raised my hand, and as there were no other volunteers I was appointed to the position of Chair that same night.

I met two Jewish women who were doing philanthropic work at the Voluntary Service Council who provided me with an office, a desk and chair, an index card box, and a phone. So I began to raise funds to establish the 'Brent Black Mental Health Project', considered a first across all of the UK.

The project lasted eight years but by then I had already begun a career in local government, which would continue for twenty years, before I made the momentous decision to emigrate to Australia.

Postscript

I remember many years ago as a young man coming across some unknown spiritual folk tales in a notebook at home. Were they tales from my grandmother's psyche or simply passed down the generations? Legends about seeing ghosts, headless horsemen and women, and the shocking idea of 'putting me back where you got me from' with *Le Diable*. Stories of those who sold their souls to the devil in return for earthly riches.

Looking back now on my adolescence, I see myself then as a teenage boy alone. On the threshold of his adult life, when he finds a notebook with his grandmother's stories, they make no sense. He tries by the light of the moon to decipher what could have been Delphic sayings, delivered with a big dose of Trinidadian irony.

Frustrated, he throws the notebook down. His elders' language makes no sense to him and he vows he shall not use it. He won't tell them he's going to make a long journey – and the less they know, the better for them and him. It will keep them safe from knowledge if he's captured by the forces of the state, principally the police or those doctors in white coats who may say he is mad and bad.

He looks in the mirror and thinks, *I look ugly. Why can't I disguise myself with white paint? Anything to remove the stig-mata of dark skin!* The boy-man decides to tackle the suffocating silence of nights at home to give his dreams a chance of survival, for that silence will only lead to death. So he travels through a forbidding terrain, the dark nights and treacherous landscapes of London.

Many years later when someone tells him he cares for him – loves him – the nightmare of that distant journey returns to haunt him, even though the fact that love can occur in ordinary circumstances does not cause him to wonder. A friend is driving him and his close friend as they sit together in the back seat, as usual.

He becomes aware of a rising irritation and utters a thought that must have been ripped from that early notebook. 'I never want to be a back street driver'. It's as if he's in imminent danger from those same unseen dark night forces.

His intimate friend's response is dry. 'Oh, really? You do surprise me!'

With a roar of laughter, the fear is dispelled by humour and they arrive at their appointment without mishap.

But back when I was a young pimply schoolboy, despite my impatience I would stand loyally to attention, listening as my father sketched out his story-thinking. It seemed to me that he didn't care for me at all. I was an empty vessel to be filled with his hopes and dreams, whether I understood it or not. Words by the hundred woven into stories with ghosts, women leading men astray, untrustworthy parents and grandparents, duty, responsibility, all told with inscrutable pride as my mother looked on.

Was that disdain I saw play across her lips as she silently rebuked a man who could not deliver all that he had promised?

That man who had stood waiting for her at the quayside. Who had stood waiting for his infant son too. Who grew to know me and love me but didn't know how to express his love directly to me.

Eventually it was time for me to escape all the obligations to my parents, and tender brotherly love, eating Auntie's Christmas cake, and trying to understand death. I decided twenty – a nice round figure – would be the suitable age to act. Duties discharged, education survived. Either to leave or fake it, with happy smiling parents, admiring friends and a family of my own. The only other alternative to avoid that fate was dying.

My notes – my diary stories – were my light for escape. What my grandparents did and said, where we came from, even the words: 'The United States of America' stirred my sensibility. It was a gradual awakening to where my roots were. My grandparents had had a link with, and an understanding of, America and I came to realise that my world was bigger than Britain, a monoculture. I was discovering my identity, and could see that I had originated from a wider world. I was not just my father's creation, but I had deeper roots stretching back to Trinidad. The way my father existed, never happily integrated into white English society, was at odds with my yearning to socialise. My parents had encouraged me to accept English culture yet in their home it was a Trinidadian upbringing, but in a cold hostile climate. I understood my parents had been young once, but I never understood what they had sacrificed.

Dad would tell me during lengthy Sunday morning monologues about his life in Trinidad. There had been opposition to his marriage with Mum. It was a cascade of words that hypnotised me. For some inexplicable reason I always stood as if on a military parade ground and wanted, so wanted, to sleep. The monologue included the statements: 'I don't want my children to go to church. I want them to make up their own minds'. Yet I was being told – there was no discussion. How I longed to break the chain of silence to say what I thought!

I retreated into a private world of music during those long nights traversing hostile territory. Then just as it seemed all was lost, I glimpsed freedom's possibilities when I caught words filled with optimism and hope. Lyrics float back to me: *to be young, gifted and black*.[2] I wanted to turn up the volume of my little transistor radio, to blast it out to all my unseen foes with their evil thoughts. *I will carry on to fulfil my dreams*, I thought. Yes, music opened a door: black hearts and black voices sang words of hope to keep me going through the challenges of a childhood poisoned by racism. When Bob and Marcia announced it, you saw it take shape but I was still almost strangled by silence. Music really connected for me in those early years of a broad 1970s education. And then the 1980s, the start of a long ascent.

I tried to match my mother's words of striving and heard the words of Desmond Dekker echoing around and around in my head:

You can get it if you really want
You can get it if you really want
You can get it if you really want
But you must try, try and try, try and try
You'll succeed at last![3]

2 'Bob and Marcia' were a Jamaican vocal duo, Bob Andy and Marcia Griffiths. They had a #5 UK hit single in 1970.
3 Jamaican singer Desmond Dekker, Reggae Got Soul 1976. First released by Jimmy Cliff 1968.

That's my exclamation. The nonsense of thinking that by my brilliance alone I could succeed against all the forces determined to prevent 'Black Boy' from having my slice of life. The yearning was there but I doubted myself – nervous, silent and fearful of retribution.

Yeah, there's a great truth you should know
When you're young, gifted and black
Your soul's intact ...
There are times when I look back
And I am haunted by my youth
Oh but my joy of today
Is that we can all be proud to say
To be young, gifted and black
Is where it's at.

Analysing those lyrics now seems a lifetime away from the scenes of my 'existential' anxieties in high school. The words take on a poignancy that is hard to overstate.

To be accepted as a complete and respected member of the human race. Was that too much to ask?

FROM THE SAME PUBLISHER

A Taste for Diamonds

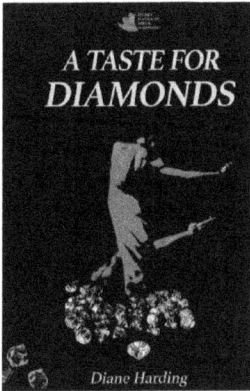

A diamond theft. A fateful dancer. Passion, love and money in a story that unfolds through the rhythm of the tango.

'A Taste for Diamonds' is a love story that spans two continents, from London to Buenos Aires, as Harriett and the man she loves – the man who loves her in return – face the consequences of getting involved in the international diamond trade.

Not everyone's a good guy, as they find out to their peril.

Author **Diane Harding** plumbs the depths of romance and intrigue to bring readers a satisfying ending to a dangerous tale of love.

Category: BOOKS – MYSTERY – THRILLER – CRIME

An extraordinary relationship

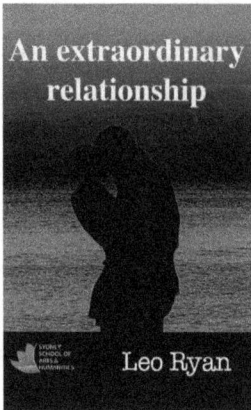

An extraordinary
relationship

Leo Ryan

Early in **Leo Ryan**'s career as a counsellor he became aware of the number of female clients being abused by their husbands/partners/boyfriends and was determined to help.

This book highlights his conclusions, making it possible for most people to bring on the changes needed have a great relationship.

Category: NON-FICTION – HOW-TO BOOK
             RELATIONSHIPS

Burma My Mother
And Why I Had To Leave

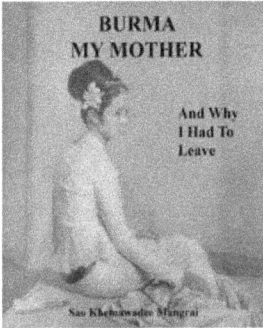

Myanmar's future is informed by its past - and BURMA MY MOTHER tells it like it is. A valuable story of living through good times and plenty of bad in Burma, now known as Myanmar, before an escape to a new life of freedom.

Author **Sao Khemawadee Mangrai**'s husband, Hom, was imprisoned for 5 years, and his father was shot and killed sitting alongside independence leader, General Aung San, when he was assassinated.

Khemawadee grew up in a Shan state in the north-east of Myanmar, previously known as Burma, and now lives in Sydney. Her sad memories are also infused by the beauty of the country and the grace of Myanmar's Buddhist culture.

Category: MEMOIR

Drenched
by the Sun

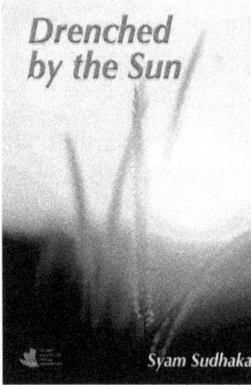

I, who prophesy
by reading the stars and the wind,
now think of that country ...

Syam Sudhakar 'has an eye for the strange and the uncanny and a way of building translucent metaphors,' according to leading South Indian poet, K. Satchidanandan.

An award-winning poet who writes in English and Malayalam, Sudhakar is based in Kerala, teaching and researching Indian poetry.

Category: POEMS

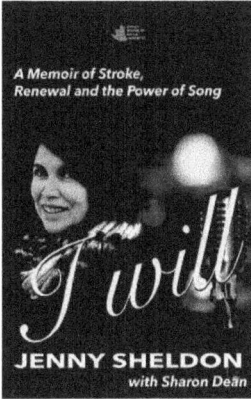

I WILL

Unable to speak after suffering a stroke, **Jenny Sheldon** never lost her understanding of words.

Determined to regain her life, she used singing, swimming and her love of life to find her way back. This book is her triumph – and a compelling example to others.

Category: MEMOIR

Jiddu Krishnamurti World Philosopher
Revised Edition

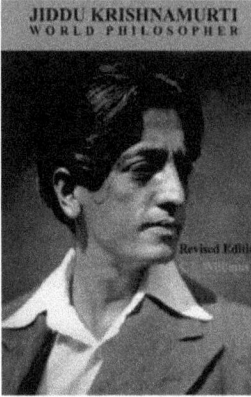

The life of the 20th-century philosopher Jiddu Krishnamurti was truly astonishing. As this new updated edition shows, people from all over the world would gather to hear him speak the wisdom of the ages.

Biographer **Christine (CV) Williams** carried out research over a period of four years to write this ebook account of Krishnamurti's life. She studied his major archive of personal correspondence and talks, and interviewed people who knew him intimately.

Krishna was born into poverty in a South Indian village, before being adopted by a wealthy English public figure, Annie Besant. As an adult he settled in California, travelling to India and England every year to give public lectures that inspired spiritual seekers beyond any single religion.

Category: BIOGRAPHY

Night Road to Life

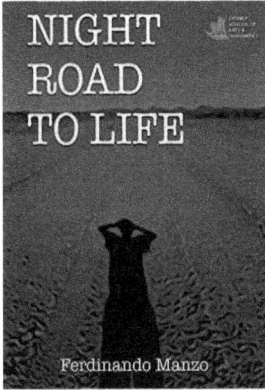

Themes of the sea and the emotions, particularly the deeply felt joys and melancholies experienced by men, are a touchstone of NIGHT ROAD TO LIFE.

Ferdinando Manzo's thoughts are not bound to fluidity; they fly to the greatest heights of exhilaration in poems such as, *The sky above us*, which displays 'a mantle of stars that burns in my heart' and in the evocative lines of *Eclipse*: 'the moon rose, bright between the eyelids of the night'.

Even the constellation Andromeda is given due recognition, breaking her chains and ready for revenge, before another poem *The voice of the universe* explores 'a hidden legend as far away as waves in outer space'.

A distinctive quality of this collection of poems is its musicality – the sounds of words carefully chosen, and their rhythms. The pleasing effect of the sensuality of sounds, ranging from gentleness to the drama of sex, is in tune with the gamut of human emotion.

Category: POEMS

Reported Missing

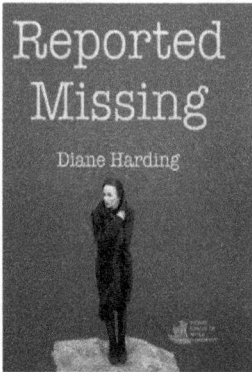

Di Harding's novel is set in a very contemporary Sydney, taking in multi-layered sights and sounds, from the northern beaches to performances at the Sydney Opera House.

The plot spans the complications of what a woman must consider if she is to save her children from domestic violence. And the main character has good reason to hold fears for her life.

What would you do if your daughter was missing and you thought your son-in-law was somehow involved? Is there someone who could help you, or would you take matters into your own hands?

She does, and so the terror begins – from vile and personal harassment to life threatening acts, until she is ready to commit murder.

Her obsession with killing grows in her mind until she begins to plan and plot. Can she actually do it? Then something shocking happens to make up her mind.

The story ends on an upbeat for a new life ahead for the family.

Category: DOMESTIC VIOLENCE
CRIME FICTION – SYDNEY NOVEL
AUSTRALIAN FICTION

Road
to Mandalay
Less Travelled

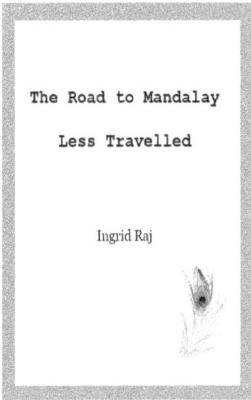

The Road to Mandalay

Less Travelled

Ingrid Raj

'The Road to Mandalay Less Travelled' by **Ingrid Raj** provides research on a selection of Anglo-Burmese writing published from the period of British rule in Burma up until 2007.

What Raj shares with us in this study is the knowledge she gained about the value of social resistance achieved through writing. Both fiction and non-fiction texts are included in arguing a case that these might be viewed as tools of often ambivalent resistance against oppressive regimes, both local and colonial.Her research deserves a wider readership than was initially provided, and to this aim Sydney School of Arts & Humanities presents the work as its first publication in this new category of Essays & Theses.

We hope that specialist researchers as well as members of the general reading public take this opportunity to learn more about the culture of the people of Myanmar through their unique approach to storytelling, based largely on their religious understanding, their rich store of folk legend and their chequered history.

Category: MEMOIR – LITERATURE – BURMA – HISTORY

Road to Rishi Konda

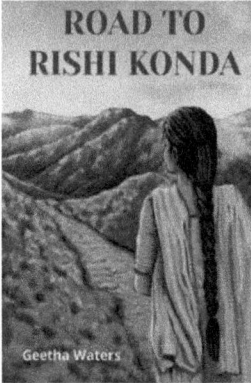

'ROAD TO RISHI KONDA' by **Geetha Waters** is a memoir of insight and charm, with a serious educational purpose. The author recalls delightful and stimulating stories from her childhood to throw light on the work of the philosopher J. Krishnamurti as a revolutionary 20th century educator.

At once fascinating and enchanting, Geetha Waters' stories centre on a girl growing up in Kerala and Andhra Pradesh in the '60s and '70s.

These youthful tales are underpinned by Geetha's deep understanding of childhood education, based both on her academic studies and in practice in her daily life as a mother and childcare professional.

Written from a child's perspective, the tales of awakening to life offer the reader an opportunity to appreciate how all children learn, as they draw on a deep well of curiosity that needs to be respected.

Category: BIOGRAPHY & AUTOBIOGRAPHY
PERSONAL MEMOIR – EDUCATORS

Stranger

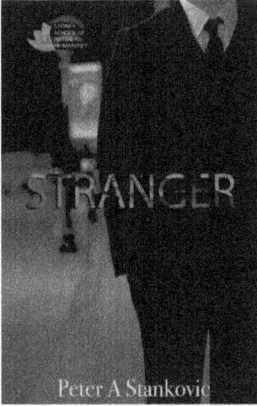

Political journalist Nick Hunter suddenly loses his memory. He can't find his wallet, his computer password or even his name. When it comes to women it's even more confusing. Does he have a lover or a wife?

It doesn't get any easier when he realises his life is in danger as he's been researching a story on corruption at the highest level of political life. Things get even stickier once Nick has a 6-shooter out of his safety deposit box and in his hand, ready to fire in his own defence.

Set in the northern and eastern suburbs of Sydney where coffee and sex are almost too freely available, this story will sharpen your senses and set your crime thriller compass on true course.

Category: FICTION – CRIME

The Boots

All Mike has to do is get his mate's lucky boots to the stadium – but when Mike accidentally loses them his day is turned upside down.
Will he find them – and if so, will it be in time for the game?

In trying to meet the deadline, Mike has to cope with weekend crowds, hamburger cravings, a girl with a fox tattoo, Jedi Knights, and a bunch of footie supporters who are hell bent on getting their hands on those lucky boots.

Mike always thought Karma was a myth. But he may just become a believer.

Category: FICTION – ACTION & ADVENTURE – SPORTS & RECREATION – RUGBY LEAGUE

The Dark Side of the Opera

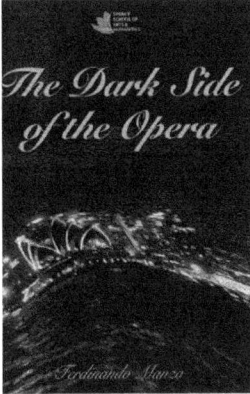

In this collection, **Ferdinando Manzo** plays with language, teasing out meaning and tempting the senses. His poetic approach is akin to the Buddhist path where happiness is gained through an understanding of negation.

From the earthly to the stellar, each poem holds the reader in suspense until the final moment.

Category: POEMS

Waking the Mind

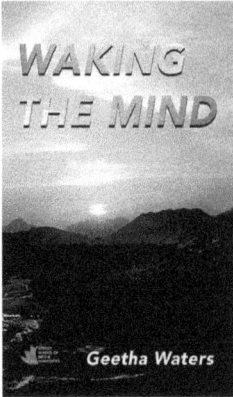

Geetha Waters' engaging selection of short stories, 'Waking the Mind', is a reflection on Jiddu Krishnamurti's impact on her education based on her experiences at a school he founded in South India.

Geetha credits her passion for inquiry as being sparked the first time she heard Krishnamurti speak when she was six. That talk at the Rishi Valley School set her on an intriguing course of inquiry into the mysterious nature of the mind, the vitality of the natural world, and a creative understanding of life.

'Waking the Mind' is Geetha Waters' second book, following Road to Rishi Konda, her stories of a girl growing up in Kerala and Andhra Pradesh in the '60s and '70s.

Geetha Waters also incorporates the stories found in 'Road to Rishi Konda' in the STEP program for children and teachers in South India, a training module based on Krishnamurti's interactive style of relating with children.

Category: NON-FICTION – INDIAN STORIES – PHILOS OPHY KRISHNAMURTI

What's in a Name?
20 People - 20 Stories

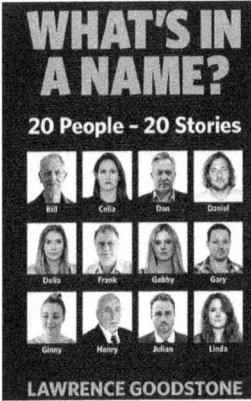

This collection of short stories will appeal to readers who are attracted to snapshots of the human condition. While set in Australia, the stories reflect universal themes. They range over a number of genres from crime to science fiction, from human weakness to human strength, and capture pockets of life with uncanny accuracy and sensitivity.

The author, **Lawrence Goodstone**, is a retired public servant who spent his professional life writing for others. With a background ranging from teaching to immigrant services as well as assisting in the delivery of the 2000 Olympic Games in Sydney, he is now in a position to write for himself and create stories from a life well lived.

Category: FICTION – SHORT STORY – SYDNEY STORIES
AUSTRALIAN FICTION